LOST PERTHSHIRE

Ann Lindsay

BIRLINN

First published in 2011 by
Birlinn Ltd
West Newington House
10 Newington Road
Edinburgh
EH9 1QS

www.birlinn.co.uk

ISBN 978 84158 557 4

British Library Cataloguing-in-Publication Data
A catalogue record for this book is available
from the British Library

Series design by Mark Blackadder

Typeset by Brinnoven, Livingston
Printed and bound by Gutenberg Press, Malta

*To William, born in 2010 and
already an explorer of Perthsire*

CONTENTS

ACKNOWLEDGEMENTS
AND PICTURE CREDITS

Lost Perthshire has been written from information acquired from innumerable sources, including: Andrew Simmons of Birlinn whose patience is beyond that of a saint; Jane Anderson, Archivist at Blair Castle, Atholl Estates for information and the use of images; Jane Banner, who wrote *The Braes of Tullymet*, and the A.K. Bell Library who produced the book; Professor Gordon J. Barclay, who generously allowed me to quote extensively from his extensive research about the WW II defence lines in Scotland; Angus Cameron and his mother, Mrs Anne Cameron, who offered not only copious amounts of information and lunch but also gave permission to use photos of Mrs Cameron's early water-skiing ventures on Loch Earn; Peter Clarke for information on extinct animals; Sue Cole, from Meigle, who took me on a conducted tour of the area, and whose book on Meigle gave much information; Anthony Cooke, who wrote *A History of Redgorton Parish*; Kirsty Dicken for loan of several books on Perthshire; Jeremy Duncan, for information about market crosses and the proposed Perthshire canal; Dunkeld Chapter House Museum and Archives for information about the Perthshire Fencibles and the use of many images; Mrs Elizabeth Fleming for her account of her time at Rannoch School, published on www.exrannoch.com; Miss Rhoda Fothergill, who offered use of her booklet, 'The Waterways of Perth', produced with the schoolchildren at the Caledonian School, Perth; Geoff Holder, whose generously offered me the use of so many of his photos; Thomas Huxley, who gave me time to answer my queries about Thomas Graham of Lynedoch; Allan Knaik, who offered the images of Clathymore control tower; Norman McCandlish for the loan of several out of print books, and much information about Strathtay; Professor John M. MacKenzie of Alyth; Sir William Macpherson of Cluny for information about his family; Market

Harborough Royal British Legion for the story of Bernard Hallsall MC; Alf Marshall of the Dunning Parish Historical Society; Felicity Martin, who gave much information about the Coronation Road; James Miller for allowing us to quote from his book on the building of the hydro-electric dams in Scotland, *The Dambuilders*; Donald Paton, who wrote *Twixt Castle and Mart*; Rosalind and Peter Pearson for the generous loan of the Stobie maps of 1783; Perth and Kinross Heritage Trust; Suki Urquhart for permission to use sections for her article on Tin (corrugated iron) Houses; Ian Sinclair of Dunkeld for information on the travels of the Dunkeld Market Cross; Jess Smith, for information on schools for Travellers; Thomas Smyth, Archivist at the Black Watch Museum for much information and illustrations about the Black Watch Regiment; Neil Ramsay, Heritage Paths Project Officer, Scottish Rights of Way and Access Society in Edinburgh; Harry Rigby, for permission to use his photos of old cinemas in Blairgowrie and Coupar Angus; also Gordon Barr, Jim Brooks, Alex Braid and George Miller for information on old cinemas; Dr Lindsey J. Thomson of Robert Gordon University for much information on Market crosses; Andrew Tosh, who generously supplied information and all photographs of Lochton House; Graeme Watson of the Perth Society of Natural Science; Mrs. Jean Wilson, who responded to my request to identify the location of a building depicted in an untitled photo, circa 1880 (she recognized the building as the Bailie Nicol Jarvie Hotel in Aberfoyle, which no longer operates as a hotel); the late Dr Mary Young, who not only wrote copiously about Pitmiddle, but also accompanied me to the site, and gave generously of her time and knowledge (I have quoted from an article she produced 'A Short History of Pitmiddle'.)

I am also grateful for having been able to quote material from the following websites:

www. archaeologydataservice.ac.uk
www.bgk.org.uk
www.dundee.ac.uk/
www.exrannoch.com
www.geograph.org.uk
www.glasgowsculpture.com
www.molrs.org.uk
www.pkht.org.uk
www.polishresettlementcampsintheuk.co.uk

www.robroycountry.com
www.scottishaeroclub.org.uk
www.scottisharchitects.org.uk
www.scottishcinemas.org.uk
www.scottish-places.info/towns
www.secretscotland.org.uk
www.1st-mac.com/
www.wartimememories.co.uk/ships/

Ann Lindsay
Meikle Trochry
September 2011

PICTURE CREDITS

Blair Castle Archives, pp. 58, 80, 81, 91, 104, 105, 131, 140, 192
Angus and Mrs Anne Cameron, p. 191
Aileen Kellie, pp. 118, 119, 125, 126, 145, 180, 182, 185, 190
Allan Knaik, p. 37
Dunkeld Museum and Archives, pp. 28, 29, 30
Geoff Holder, pp. 9, 12, 34, 35, 36, 53, 54, 122
James Miller, p. 66
Perth and Kinross Library, p. 43
Perth Museum and Art Gallery, pp. 51, 61, 73, 78, 96, 97
Peter Pearson, pp. 87, 102, 114, 155
Harry Rigby, pp. 195, 197
Andrew Tosh, p. 100
All other images are from the author's collection

INTRODUCTION

Stroll for a few paces on Perthshire soil and glance behind at your very own footprints. Chances are that wherever you are, or wherever you step, you may well be treading precisely where illustrious predecessors have trod, where armies have marched or where generations have tilled the soil with superhuman energy to improve much of the land.

Few areas of Scotland can boast of such a myriad of powerful people of diverse backgrounds and determinations, who did not just pass by, using Perthshire as a staging post, but looked around, judged this a good place in which to live, and settled down. Today it is not only the natural beauty of the land, but also the benefits of man-made improvements and the imprint of inspired architecture which impress inhabitants and visitors.

Picts, Romans, kings and queens, dukes, political heavyweights, engineering giants, Jacobites, prisoners of war, witches, literary heroes, and fearsome Highlanders with their cattle have all tramped on Perthshire soil and, in some way, have left their mark. Those who pitched their camps or erected shelters, those who built and lived in castles or rudimentary cottages, sturdy farm houses and even a royal palace: of such varied human efforts Perthshire was created.

Kings were once crowned here at Scone. The almost forgotten route which they took from Edinburgh is described later in this book. The routes by which commoners tramped the land and which have almost been lost are also retraced. Invaders have been few, but defensive measures have been remarkably frequent.

Wild animals such as bears, aurochs, wolves, beavers, goats and boars which roamed this county have long been banished or exterminated, so no longer wander our wilderness unfettered and at will. Little is evident of Iron Age forts, mysterious stone circles, cup stones and crannogs which hide under the earth or the lochs of Perthshire.

Dealing as it does with a county with so much evidence of human habitation, and with such a long and varied history, this book can only be a tantalising overview, a dip into the kaleidoscope of historical detail, rather than a comprehensive document. While much of Perthshire's tangible heritage has vanished or remains half-hidden, it need not be lost entirely. The essence of 'Lost Perthshire' is to uncover the wealth of its history for posterity, and to revel in the wonderful landscape, both natural and man-made.

CHAPTER 1

BURGEONING BOUNDARIES, VANISHING VILLAGES AND FEUDAL RULE

Perthshire has been known for some decades as 'the big County'. Today, its 5,800 square kilometres contain wild moorland, such as Rannoch in the west, high mountain ranges in the north, and rich farmlands in the lower lands of the rivers Tay, Earn and Isla. But just when Perthshire became known as a 'shire', and was initially and clearly defined as such, is lost in the mists of time. From where did these boundaries evolve? How did Perthshire end up being the geographical entity it is today? And which areas were annexed in its long history, or dropped off in various reorganisations? The answers are often surprising, vague and confusing.

The definition and boundaries of many Scottish counties developed slowly and haphazardly from the various areas controlled by local stewartries (from which the surname Stewart is derived), or sheriffdoms, of the sixteenth and seventeenth centuries. Until this point, justice was mostly under the control of the local laird and landowner, who meted out punishments more or less as he saw fit. This was clearly cherished as a right by most powerful landowners as they could effectively rule as kings within their own fiefdom, and had power over life and death. Their jurisdiction within their areas, therefore, created boundaries.

Some further clues about the early boundaries might lie within the writings of John of Fordoun, a man of the Church. (The 'Fordoun' refers not, it appears, to his surname but to the area of the Mearns in what used to be Kincardineshire.) He wrote in the latter part of the fourteenth century, and his writings are generally accepted to be the first known history of Scotland. Legend has it that he was angered by the removal of the Scottish national records to England by

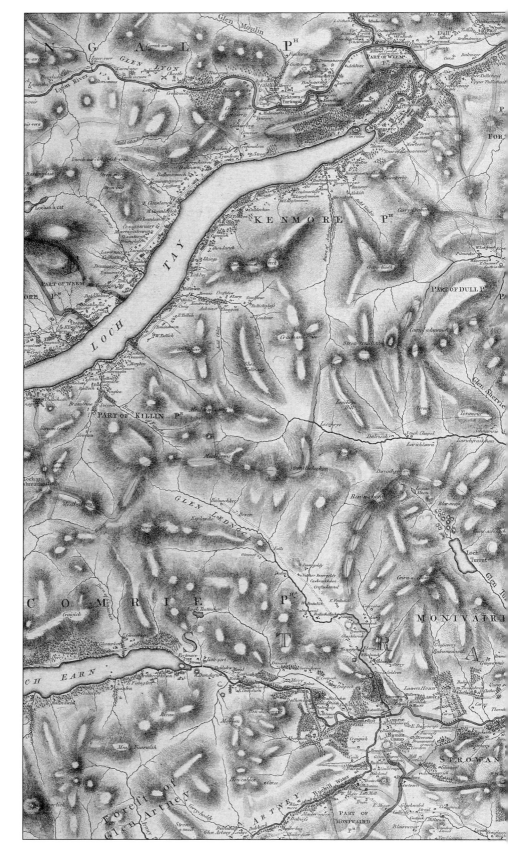

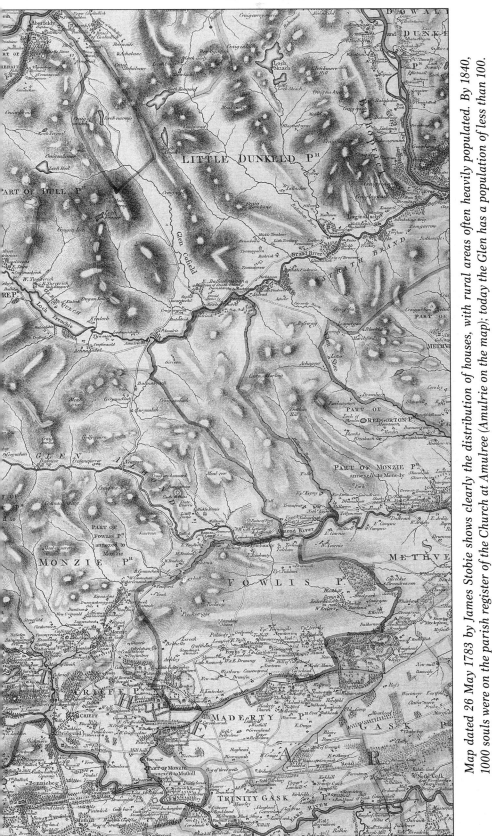

Map dated 26 May 1783 by James Stobie shows clearly the distribution of houses, with rural areas often heavily populated. By 1840, 1000 souls were on the parish register of the Church at Amulree (Amulree on the map); today the Glen has a population of less than 100.

Edward III, so he responded by recording what he discovered about Scottish history, and it is his account which states that King Malcolm II introduced not only the shire to Scotland, but also the thane class. Shires are certainly mentioned in charters by the time of the reign of King Malcolm III, who was king of Scots from 1005 until his death in 1034.

The concerted development of these shires, or sheriffdoms, can be attributed to David, King of Scots from 1124 to 1153. David's reforming influence, which oversaw the foundation of monasteries, the introduction of feudalism and the creation of small areas known as burghs, came to be known as the 'Davidian revolution', an expression still much used today.

After the Union of the Crowns in 1707, the Royal Burgh of Perth was originally a section of the Perth burghs. The burghs of Fife and Forfarshire were also included under the umbrella of the Royal Burgh of Perth. Before 1707, Commissioners from the burghs could represent multiple counties. As a result of one change which followed the 1707 Union, eight counties were paired together, electing a member at alternating elections to the unreformed House of Commons in London. The remainder of the county returned a single member as the parliamentary county of Perthshire. The parishes of Tulliallan, Culross, Muckhart, and the Perthshire portions of the parishes of Logie and Fossoway were annexed to the constituency of Clackmannanshire and Kinross in 1832 as a result of the Great Reform Act of that year.

But there still existed some strange anomalies to the boundaries of Perthshire which we see today. Prior to the 1890s, Perthshire's boundaries were irregular, and accommodated outlying, totally separate and quite distant islands within other counties. The parishes of Culross and Tulliallan formed an outpost and enclave some miles away from the rest of the county, on the boundaries of Clackmannanshire and Fife; while the northern part of the parish of Logie formed an enclave of Stirlingshire within the county of Perthshire.

Following the recommendations of the boundary commission appointed under the Local Government (Scotland) Act 1889, Culross and Tulliallan were transferred to Fife, and the entire parish of Logie and Kippen was included in Stirlingshire.

Prior to these changes, the boundaries of Perthshire formed a bewildering, wriggling edge to the county. The changes make perfect sense when studying the maps created by James Stobie in 1783 which illustrate with clarity just how uneven and irregular were the boundaries of Perthshire at that time.

To create a more orderly Perthshire boundary, parishes which straddled two of the existing counties of Perthshire and Fife, Abernethy on the borders of Fife were now included within Perthshire. Parishes such as Alyth, Coupar Angus and Kettins, which had previously been on the boundaries of Perthshire and Forfarshire, were now included wholly in Perthshire. Fowlis Easter, originally within Perthshire, but which for ecclesiastical and education purposes had been joined with the Forfarshire parish of Lundie, which had always been situated outside the boundary of Perthshire, was now transferred into Forfarshire.

Between 1890 and 1975, Perthshire was governed by its local County Council, which was enlarged by the addition of Kinross-shire in 1930. In 1975, Perthshire and Kinross-shire ceased to exist as such and were split up between Central and Tayside regions. All is now changed again, so for the moment Perth combined with Kinross is represented as an entity, although each carefully retains its distinct and separate name. Of 'Perthshire', we have once again lost sight in official parlance. The locally produced newspaper, the *Perthshire Advertiser*, and Perthshire Tourist Information preserve the name, however, as well as many local businesses which continue to use 'shire' in their names.

Just as the boundaries and names were reshaped over the centuries, so areas of population shifted, waxed and waned. Over the last few centuries this has been reflected in the findings of the Perth and Kinross Historic Environment Records, and in the listings of Scheduled Monuments.

Early maps such as the Stobie map of 1783 show Perthshire dotted with dwellings, as though every possible piece of land which could produce any type of crop was settled and exploited. Until the clearances of the early and mid-nineteenth century, for example in Glen Quaich between Amulree and Loch Tay, the local church of Amulree could claim 1,000 on its parish register. Today, there could be fewer than 10 per cent of that number populating the area.

The composition of habitations in Perthshire has changed much over the centuries, marked by a drift of population to towns, as in

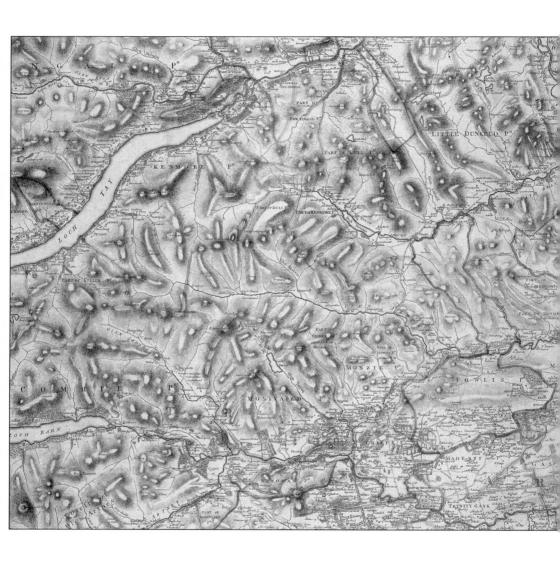

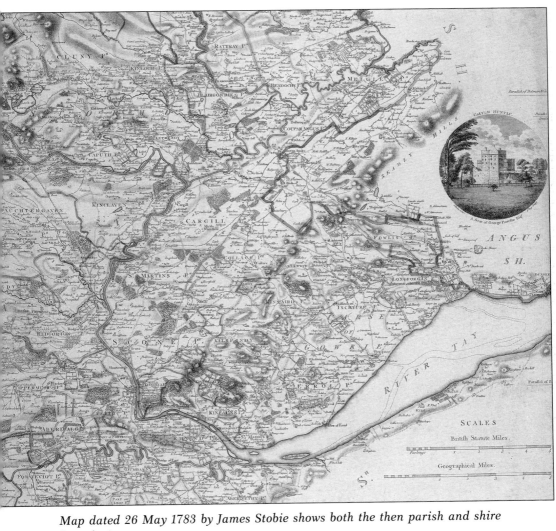

Map dated 26 May 1783 by James Stobie shows both the then parish and shire boundaries.

other parts of Scotland. Rural living has declined massively, as is indicated by at least 340 sites scattered all over Perthshire which are noted by the Perth and Kinross Historic Environment Records as having evidence of buildings. Many of these sites must have housed at least one family, and perhaps significantly more. Described as 'townships', they ranged in size from a large farm with corn mill and other farm buildings, to a hamlet which might contain a school, smiddy, mill, lime kiln and associated buildings. Where a considerable number of people lived and worked, today, all are gone and the farms and hamlets are deserted. Of the many sites, there are around 20 which are now noted as being of special interest, and are protected by Scheduled Monument status, which means they are deemed to be nationally significant.

Tracing these Scheduled Sites makes fascinating reading, even if clues are sparse and tinged with folklore memories. At Fossoway, the Parks of Aldie, or 'the Muckle Toon', was identified from RAF aerial photographs taken in 1946. Quite possibly it is the site of a medieval village, connected with Aldie Castle which is now restored and inhabited. Of the village, or its size, little is known.

The extent of some of these deserted villages varies considerably. Craignavar lies close to Fowlis Wester, and contains the remains of at least 15 rectangular structures, a corn-drying kiln with associated stone-walled enclosures, and fields. Buildings also varied considerably in size, and some were divided into two or three compartments. A typical building was 23 metres by 5.5 metres and stood at a maximum height of 3 metres: a structure of considerable footprint, and roughly the size of a village hall.

Overlooking the 17-mile-long stretch of Loch Tay, a township of some substance remains, but in ruins. The buildings lie below the present-day church of Lawers on the A827, not far from the shoreline and opposite Ardtalnaig, which is on the south side of the loch. This village consisted of a laird's house, a church constructed in 1669, two mills, nine other buildings, a corn-drying kiln, mill lade, bridge, a number of enclosures and a possible ice house. With such proximity to the loch, and this offering the easiest method of transportation, it was not surprising that a pier was also found. As in the case of so many old buildings, much stone would have been taken away to be reused, and between an earlier mapping of the district by a surveyor called John Farquharson in 1769, and later finds, some buildings

Ruins are all that remains of the hamlet close to Newton Bridge in the Sma'
Glen, just off the A822 running from Amulree to Crieff.

would have been built on different sites in the eighteenth and
nineteenth centuries.

Kerrowmore officially lies within the civil parish of Fortingall,
but is some distance up the River Lyon from the charming, thatched
Fortingall village. Kerrowmore is close to the Bridge of Balgie, on
the south side of the river, and at the junction of the road leading to
Meggernie Castle and the road south over to Loch Tay. The evidence
here of early occupation is described by the Perth and Kinross
Heritage Trust as being 'an unusual earthwork on top of a rocky
knowe, consisting of two concentric terraces, the upper of which
is 2.5 metres wide enclosing the D-shaped summit which measures
24 metres by 12 metres and around which are traces of a very slight

bank'. Surrounding this knoll are seven buildings. Kerrowmore lies within a highly picturesque setting, seen through the car windows of twenty-first century visitors, but its strategic position must surely tell a tale. Only rumour, though, links this with 'Black John of the Spears', a shadowy character who might also have been named John of Lorne, and lived around the mid-sixteenth century during the lawless cattle-stealing era.

The evocatively-named Reinakyllich, which lies officially in the civil parish of Moulin, north of Pitlochry, is, in fact, three miles or so up Glen Girnaig from Killiecrankie. Of this cluster of buildings, around eight roofed buildings, two enclosures, a lime kiln and a head dyke used to separate cultivated ground from grazing grounds, are mapped. Further west, in an area which holds many more deserted farm townships, is one substantial cluster of buildings intriguingly described by Scheduled Monument records as 'an island of rough pasture, surrounded by heather moorland' containing remains called 'chapel' or 'chapelton' in Glen Banvie. This collection numbers 22 buildings and three enclosures, and was probably depopulated in the 1850s.

Many ruins at which walkers and tourists may simply glance, or whizz past within a few strides, have even more ancient history. Within spitting distance of the visitor centre overlooking Loch Tummel are the remains of an Iron Age homestead about 2,000 years old, enclosed by a circular wall 3 metres thick and with an overall diameter of about 25 metres. Driving further west for just over a mile on the B8019, one arrives at Borenich, a collection of buildings, one of which was noted on the first edition Ordnance Survey map as being occupied in the mid-nineteenth century. However, within one building is a small hole in the floor which gives access into a well-constructed, vaulted cellar built of small stones quite unlike those visible above ground. This suggests to today's surveyors that the building might well have been of a relatively high status. Hugh Mitchell, who in 1923 wrote *Pitlochry District – its Topography, Archaeology and History*, became exuberant at this discovery, even suggesting that the vaulting 'was very fine and of small brick-like stones, similar to that in the chancel of St Giles Church in Edinburgh, and if of the same period would be c.1450'. However, later suggestions are more prosaic, and it has been deemed to be a potato clamp, or store. Again, within a few strides of the road and virtually within sight of Borenich, about 750

Harvesting in the 1880s high up on the North side of Loch Tay, when the area was more populated with small hamlets and farm townships than today.

metres westwards and overlooking Loch Tummel, is the substantial township of the tongue-twisting Bail a Chaisteal or Bail A' Chaisted, with twelve buildings.

One of the largest remains of houses and a village is at Ballinloan. The habitation of Salachill lies on a south-facing hill overlooking the Ballinloan Burn and at one time consisted of 23 buildings, of which some are still roofed. A thriving village community once inhabited this area, and indeed there was an inn. The size of the farm buildings indicates just how prosperous the farming must have been here. In one of the farm buildings, although the exact one is not accurately known, lived Kitty Macdonald.

Beatrix Potter recorded conversations with Kitty Macdonald, who was to be the model for Mrs Tiggy-Winkle. Kitty had been a washer-woman for the Potter family when they had spent their holidays

Remains of limekilns are dotted round the county. This one in the Sma' Glen is still recognizable, although obscured by the growth of turf.

at Dalguise. She was by this time 83, but Beatrix Potter recalled she was

> . . . waken and delightfully merry . . . a comical round little old woman, as brown as a berry and wears a multitude of petticoats and a white 'mutch'.
>
> When she was seven years old she went to 'my uncle Prince', who had a farm a mile up the water from Ballinloan, as a herd, and remained with him eight years herding the cattle on the hills.
>
> Kitty must have had a frugal life always, but she dwelt on this early part as a time of positive privation. Apart from the hardship, she spoke with affection of the idyllic shepherd life in summer on the hills. They milked the ewes then, a thing a crofter would hardly condescend to now.

What did they live on? Just meat and a little milk. 'Aye thae were potatoes but no money; aye neeps'. The staple evidently porridge. 'They wad kill a sheep sometimes, or a stirk.' She mentioned pigs as a source of satisfactory profit.

They were content to wear the coarse worsted of their own flocks, their scanty stock of hand-spun linen lasted practically a lifetime. According to old Kitty, Strath Braan was populous once, 'hundreds'. I could not get an exact idea, but they emigrated in a convoy as McDougal would say, to North America, 'My uncle Prince's descendants are prosperous in California', she had had a letter last week. You will scarcely find a single family in this neighbourhood who have not relations over the sea. The old crofter farms will never return. When one considered the scanty draggled crops grown in the bottoms of windy valleys, it is madness to dream of ploughing up the heather.

[1892] I talked to her again about Ballinloan, getting set right on several points. I asked how it was that General Wade had built a stone bridge in such a remote spot, and she assured me that she could remember when there was a great deal of traffic. There was actually a Dye works and Tannery at Ballinloan, and cobblers self contained. General Wade led the road through to Aberfeldy.

Beatrix Potter appears unlikely to have ventured up by Glenshee, unlike Queen Victoria, who must often have passed over the road up from Bridge of Cally towards Glenshee, and eventually arriving at Braemar and Deeside. Within the civil parish of Kirkmichael is Easter Bleaton, about five miles north of Bridge of Cally on the A93, and on the east side of the Black Water river there was a settlement of 52 buildings, grouped at the foot of the charmingly named Knockali Hill. Although little remains except the lower courses of stone, this area contained at least eight separate farmsteads, and five retting pools for the soaking of flax prior to weaving, suggesting that this was a busy village and farm area, although there is no evidence that it was as old as Arnbathie, in Kilspindie on the present-day Carse of Gowrie.

Arnbathie comprises a hamlet, or a small gathering of farms, outbuildings and enclosure, now only visible as a series of grass-covered foundations which lie to the north of the Iron Age Law hill fort within five miles, as the crow flies, east of Scone Palace. The settlement area dates back to medieval times, as evidenced by the pottery finds there. Arnbathie is suggestive of lower status, and the same could be said of another village, Pitmiddle, further to the east.

The ruined village of Pitmiddle sits in a scoop of upper hillside commanding a view of the entire Tay estuary, from St Madoes to Dundee and beyond to the hills of Fife. From the unmarked road nearby, there is no clue to its whereabouts. No signpost. Not even the most common and sole reminder of a vanished habitation: a church gable end or short bell tower. However, while so many of Perthshire's abandoned villages are also lost to history, much is now known about Pitmiddle thanks to the late Dr Mary Young, who lived close by and devoted considerable time to discovering the lengthy history of this village.

Climbing up the hill in the teeth of an almost permanent westerly wind, or worse, an easterly draught, one might start formulating clear, chilly ideas of just why Pitmiddle might be abandoned in the modern, comfort-seeking twentieth century. The Picts most probably settled here. They occupied the area of Gowrie which existed here for around 600 years, between the third and ninth centuries. After all, the Picts were tough types, having put paid to the Romans occupying the area, and were descendents of the native Iron Age tribes. Even the name of Pitmiddle is of Pictish origin.

But cresting the hill, panting and admiring the view, one then drops down into the scoop of hillside with the ruins of houses just discernible in an unstructured grouping. Walls shelter substantial bushes of redcurrants, huge yews survive and wild bluebells are abundant. But most telling of all are the colossal sycamores and their offspring, perhaps 30 feet high, which grow straight up. They are neither bent over by decades of a prevailing, merciless wind, nor deformed by broken branches. The secret reason why this habitation survived for more than 1,000 years was that this was a commanding position within a sheltered micro-climate, where the inner fields to the houses were relatively easy to cultivate, and the outer fields rich and less windswept than those of many of their neighbours. The Picts, having so much of the area to pick from, chose wisely. Pitmiddle fitted their ideal criteria, enjoying a south-facing slope on rich ground, 150–200 metres above sea level. By contrast, the low-lying Carse of Gowrie was at that time a vast bogland.

Dr Young explained that the name, although Pictish in origin, is further elucidated by the first historical reference dated 1172 in a

Pitmiddle supported a community until 1938, and this may well be the remains of one of the last houses to be occupied.

Remains of chains for farm machinery on a wall at the ruined village of Pitmiddle, around which the land was cultivated by locals inhabitants for around half a millennium.

charter of King William the Lion that grants to Ralph Rufus 'Kinnaird in its right divisions, except Petmeodhel belonging to Richard my Clerk'.

'Pet' or 'pit' represents a share, division or piece of land. Meodhel is possibly a personal name, making it 'Meodhel's share' Alternatively, it may well be a corruption of 'measdhon' which represents 'middle', or the 'middle share'.

Pitmiddle was a farming settlement, without a manor house, church, school or inn. Education and church attendance took place in nearby Kinnaird during the latter years of the village's existence. Ale was provided by the growing of bere barley, which was then brewed. When the Barony of Inchmartine was created in the medieval period, Pitmiddle formed an important section, as the cattle and sheep which belonged to the village, and which grazed on ground mainly cleared of woodland, ensured that rental income in grain or livestock was likely to be forthcoming. The area around the village was divided up into the infields and outfields, and these latter stretched up into the hills behind, where still the wide rigs can be seen, most clearly defined when snow is on the ground. The nearby Outfield Farm and Guardswell (appearing on earlier maps as Grasswell) were also attached to the village of Pitmiddle. The system was simple. The infield, adjacent to the village houses, was kept under constant cultivation, producing crops for household consumption as well as chickens and perhaps a pig. The outfields were cropped for around three years, and then livestock such as sheep and cattle occupied the fields for another three years, restoring the fertility of the ground. A herdboy would be employed to tend the animals and in 1647 Edmund Jackson, one of the tenants, was fined 10 shillings by the Kirk session for striking the 'common herd' on the Sabbath.

In the eleventh and twelfth centuries Pitmiddle, along with what is now Dundee and Longforgan, was owned by the brother of William the Lion, whose name was David, later Earl of Huntingdon, in England. Sometime before 1214, David made over Pitmiddle to his illegitimate son, Henry of Stirling, and so the ownership was passed down through inheritance until around 1400. From that time, it was variously in the hands of the Ogilvy family until 1650. From then on ownership frequently changed. It was held for one year by Covenanter general Alexander Leslie, first earl of Leven, then by Major General Overton, Oliver Cromwell's commander in Scotland for six years until 1657, when it was returned to the Leslie family. In 1717 ownership went back to the Ogilvy families of Lonmay and Rothiemay in Aberdeenshire.

The Young Pretender, Bonnie Prince Charlie, passed by and stayed the night at Fingask Castle, but it was not the penalties for supporting the Jacobite cause which brought the eventual demise of Pitmiddle. It had 55 households in 1691, but by the time of the census of 1841 only 21 remained.

Pitmiddle had supported a community for hundreds of years on the specific system of infields and outfields. Households supplemented their income by women and children weaving linen spun from the flax grown in the outfields. This winter activity could mean the difference between survival and crushing debt.

As the Industrial Revolution filtered up the country, Dundee established large-scale factories using modern machinery for weaving, undercutting the value of hand-woven linen. The extra income from small-scale village loom-weaving dissipated.

As more rural folk migrated to the towns to work in the factories and mills, so the requirement for food increased and the outfields of Pitmiddle were enclosed, centred around the two new farms in the area, Guardswell and Outfield. Grain production was more efficient this way, but it was achieved at a devastating cost to the crofting villagers of Pitmiddle, who lost, in a matter of a generation, their traditional way of making a livelihood. On the high slopes, the poorer ground was planted with trees.

By the end of the nineteenth century, the census of 1891 showed merely five crofters remained. Trees which had been planted were felled for the First World War, and the village itself was reduced to one last inhabitant, James Gillies, who left in 1938. In a poignant end to a long-standing community, his displenishment sale in January 1938 was abandoned as well, due to a snowstorm. No one could access the area with ease, as its isolation and height, so prized by the Picts for its defensive position a millennium before, proved Pitmiddle's downfall.

Pitmiddle was a small habitation unlikely to have contained a central area for meetings or markets, but at the centre of many other Perthshire towns and villages there once stood a stone mercat cross. 'Mercat' is the Scots word for market, and the market cross was the proud focus point in the centre of the village or town. In fact, many small squares, or even just an open area in the midst of the town, still carry the description of 'the cross' although the original stone cross may have vanished.

The role of the cross was multiple. Around it markets would assemble, business was conducted, proclamations were made, and all the vital news of the local area was announced. From here local people learnt of events taking place close by, which might well affect them personally; perhaps it was here they gleaned rumours or news of conflicts such as the Crusades, or what became known as the Hundred Years' War in Europe, events happening very far from home.

From the cross, local men might be called to gather and pledge allegiance to their local superior, and those mustering there would offer anything they had in the way of swords, dirks or even guns.

From here, armaments might be distributed from the local laird in preparation for war. Criminals often heard their fate by the market cross, before the days of court buildings, and punishments occasionally took place close by, where stocks might sit alongside the cross.

Market crosses were privy to the daily life of the community. While the church, of course, was the main distributor of information such as the crying of marriage banns, the announcement of christenings and funerals, and the spreading not only of the word of the gospel but the minister's opinions of the morality of the age, the market cross was the place where facts and events were proclaimed or whispered. It was the precursor to the gossip pages of the local newspaper, or television soap opera of today.

With such a vital role in the community, and the local duke, lord or landowner always mindful of his image, much care was taken in the creation of the stone crosses. The carving was frequently very fine, and reflected the investment of the local feudal lord, whose coat of arms, as well as that of the local town or burgh, was depicted on one of the sides. This was yet one more way in which the local landowner could display his influence, wealth and status in the community, and remind the local populace of his power. Much of his wealth, of course, was accumulated from his tenants, and this would contribute to the cost of the carving.

From the seventeenth century onwards, there is much evidence of elaborately carved market crosses. In 1900, J.W. Small FSA wrote a detailed account, illustrated with clear line drawings, called *Scottish Market Crosses,* which listed twelve crosses still visible and standing in Perthshire. Although not comprehensive, the list marked a watershed-time in the survival of the crosses. It appears today that just three crosses stand on their original sites. Dr Lindsey J. Thomson, from Robert Gordon University, has written about the crosses in Scotland.

Historically, the market cross was the symbol of a burgh's right to trade and was located centrally in the town's market place. Documentary evidence suggests that this monument type existed by at least the 12th century in Scotland, although it is thought that these early examples were wooden. Many of the standing examples date from the 16th and 17th century, but there are also several more elaborate Victorian examples. Some burghs are recorded as having more than one market cross according to the produce sold around their base. Documentary evidence, particularly in town council records, also refers to all manner of announcements, celebrations and grisly punishments carried out at the market cross, prompting Small (1900, 5) to describe their site as *'the dreaded theatre of public punishment and shame'*! Today they are a symbol of the burgh's heritage, often seen, little contemplated.

Morphologically, the essential element of the market cross is not a cross, but a shaft crowned with an appropriate heraldic or religious emblem. Heraldic beasts (such as the unicorn or lion), armorial bearings and sundials are popular subjects of sculpture for the capital and finial of market crosses. Few actual cross-shapes appear as finials, and where they occur they tend to be stylised. Typically, the earlier, more simple constructions consist of a polygonal shaft with capital and finial, rising from a solid, stepped base. Some of the later examples are more elaborate, according to the available funding within the burgh for their construction. There are five standing examples of the round tower-based type. These consist also of a shaft crowned with capital and finial, surmounting an under structure which can be in the form of either an open, vaulted under structure or a tower with internal stairs providing access to an elevated, parapeted platform. Later, Victorian, examples are often based upon a square-shaped pedestal, sometimes tiered, and usually with quite elaborate carving. All of these types tend to be of sandstone.

Of the twelve crosses documented by Small in his book, few remain. Some have been removed from their original site. Some have been replaced by replica constructions. Bodies such as Perth and Kinross Heritage Trust have recorded many of the crosses. They have also noted whether the cross still stands as the centre of a village's or town's life. Sadly, not one now appears to play any active role. Of the 'lost' crosses, most have been moved into shelter, as a curiosity of history, preserved in public buildings. Of the stances upon which they sat, again few remain. Like so many ready-cut stones, they must have been seized for use in new buildings.

Only three ancient Perthshire crosses remain standing in their original positions, but although they still exist they have decayed to such an extent that their wonderful carvings and meaning have largely vanished. The weather-worn cross at Meikleour, dating from 1698, is surrounded by protective railings and stands outside the site of the last shop and post office. Inspected in 1940, it was described as a complex stone pillar and decorated with stars and crosses, but in the twenty-first century those images are very difficult to discern.

The cross at Kinrossie is thought to date from even earlier, in 1686, and might well have been carved by the same mason. Again, much-weathered and with most of the original carving worn away, the cross stands beside the public road at the centre of the village, enclosed now by railings. A survey by the Royal Commission on the Ancient and Historical Monuments in Scotland in 1989 states that 'It consists of a stepped plinth, a shaft and moulded head (in the form of a St Andrew's cross with each arm defined by an additional moulding) and is surmounted by a ball finial. The date (1686) is no longer visible.'

The third cross lies within the old Market Place at Strowan, in the eighteenth century a busy small hamlet a couple of miles to the west of Crieff. Close to the Earn, and standing on the old road from Comrie to Crieff which ran to the south of the Earn, the market cross has the sacred initials *INRI* (for *Jesus Nazarenus Rex Judaeorum*) inscribed in fifteenth-century letters, above a weather-worn shield of arms and more letters, now illegible.

Of the remaining crosses detailed by Small, the cross at Alyth, commissioned in 1670 by James, second earl of Airlie, no longer stands in its original position, but in another part of the town, and the Dunkeld cross has had an eventful life. Situated in the central area of Dunkeld still known as 'the Cross', and standing originally where the elaborate fountain now takes pride of place, the old market cross was removed at some unrecorded time, and ended up at Dalguise House, about five miles away. There it was knocked over and broken at some point. Today, repaired and battered but still in existence, the cross is enclosed by protective glass within the Birnam Institute, about a mile away from its original site.

Crieff's market cross, erected by James Drummond, earl of Perth and Chancellor to James VII, was propped up against the wall of a public building in 1900, and is now sheltered inside the local Tourist Information building. This cross would have seen both Bonnie Prince Charlie and Cumberland pass by, and would have been at the centre of the great cattle trysts when the black cattle arrived from the west and north on the drove roads.

Coupar Angus, like Dunkeld, has an area of the town called 'the Cross', although no cross remains there. At the village of Port na Craig, Pitlochry, the 1900 account states, sadly, that the village cross was built into the gable end of a house there. The cross at Dull, was described by Small as being perhaps the oldest of all the crosses he surveyed. It was 'a rough whinstone slab' set into a stone base, but had a missing arm which had apparently been knocked off in the previous century by a passing cart. No further reference to this cross can be found and it appears to have vanished, absorbed into surrounding buildings.

The monument comprising the market cross of Kinross is located in a small public park immediately to the east of the High Street, and is of a very simple type, with the cross itself dating from the seventeenth century or earlier, although the base and steps are modern. The jougs, for holding fast those confined to the stocks as punishment, are still evident, although it is suggested they are not in their original position. The jougs were described in a dictionary of the same date as Small's account as 'an iron neck ring that constituted the old Scottish pillory'.

Scone's market cross formerly stood in the vanished village of Old Scone, and was a poignant reminder of the habitation, being all that remained when the village was moved to New Scone in 1803. In 1844 it was described as consisting of an upright pillar, 13 feet high, slightly ornamented at the top, standing on a pedestal, surrounded by steps, and gradually diminishing to a small flat octagonal stage from which the pillar rises. Around 1854, the cross was moved about 9 metres to the south of its original site to permit the construction of a carriage drive, and its bench of steps was used for building purposes.

As J.W. Small proceeded round the country gathering information for his book on market crosses, he found further evidence of their disappearance, 'There was once a market cross of Kettins, but the market has long been done away with and the cross allowed to decay, so that at the present time (1899) there only remains a square stone about 1′ in height.'

It was removed to the east end of Kettins church in 1873, and Small described the remnant there as 'a large square stone supporting an octagonal shaft 2′3″ high, which in turn supports an octagonal basin', which he concluded was probably a font.

The Longforgan cross is presumed to have been erected by Patrick Lyon, third earl of Kinghorne and first earl of Strathmore, who inherited the Castle Huntly estate in 1660. He erected a similar cross at Glamis. Made of sandstone in the late seventeenth century, it is a slim Corinthian column, about 20 feet high and surmounted by a lion, and set upon a corniced square pedestal with a wide octagonal base. Where it originally stood in the village is uncertain, but around 1790 it was removed to the policies of Huntly Castle. In 1989 it was re-erected at its present site on Longforgan's Main Street.

In parallel with the removal of the village of Scone, the village of Rossie was demolished by the seventh earl of Kinnaird, about 1795, when he was constructing a park for his new house Rossie Priory. A new village was built at Baledgarno, the parish having been previously united with Inchture in 1670. All that remains of Rossie is the old parish church and the fine market cross. Dated 1746, this cross has a unique square fluted shaft supporting two lions and two unicorns and once stood in the centre of the village. There is also a large stone used to mount horses, called the 'Loupin-on Stane', that formerly stood by the inn door. The Dundee – Perth road formerly passed through the village. It is shown on a plan of 1783, which also shows the extent of the village.

But it is the Perth market cross which is at the centre of one of the most extraordinary stories of removal and travel. The cross itself stood in the middle of the High Street between Kirkgate and Skinnergate, but the date of its carving and being placed there is uncertain. Oliver Cromwell captured Perth in 1651. As he cast around, seizing anything of which he could make use, such as stripping the turf from the North and South Inches for his fortress, he purloined all the stone he could find nearby. This included the Perth market cross, which stood on a stepped plinth, providing a convenient amount of cut stone. He ordered its stone to be used for his citadel. After the Restoration of Charles II, a replacement cross was erected in 1669, which in turn was taken down in 1765. In an extraordinary turn of events, the stone market cross next appeared at Dale House, Caithness, and then was taken back to Perthshire, but not to Perth. It was placed at Fingask Castle, where it now stands on the lawn due south of the castle. The connection between Dale House and Fingask is remarkably simple and explains the extraordinary journey of the cross which has also, undoubtedly, saved it from disappearing. The

Murray-Threipland family owned Dale House as well as Fingask Castle. The cross therefore moved with the family.

Thus it appears that only a small fraction of the market crosses of Perthshire survive, and very few in their original positions. Glancing at Stobie's maps of the 1760s (reproduced in this book) and searching out the multitude of villages and small towns, we might well surmise that many possessed their own crosses, which would have been the focal point for many a market and meeting. What has happened to the ones which have never been recorded is anyone's guess.

CHAPTER 2

ROMAN FORTS
PERTHSIRE FENCIBLES
AND POW CAMPS

The idea of an invading army arriving in Perthshire today appears far-fetched, but in 1940 this was a very real threat after the fall of Norway to the Nazis. The most rapidly built defensive lines were completed within months in an almost superhuman attempt to block any enemy advance from the north-east of Scotland, right through the Grampians and down any usable glen.

This became known as the 'Cowie line', after the Cowie river which flows eastwards to the sea near Stonehaven, and its intriguing story appears later in this chapter. But the idea of blocking glens to prevent attack from an aggressive force from the north was nothing new; nor indeed was the idea of building military roads or defensive forts. The straight roads built by the Romans can only rarely be seen or traced in Perthshire. The same applies to those constructed around 1,600 years later by General George Wade in the mid-eighteenth century. But occasionally, and principally because of the difficulties of the terrain, the Roman roads and forts, General Wade's roads, and the 1940s defensive measures almost coincide, or even overlap.

Much of the evidence of Romans in Perthshire is derived from an account of the actions and successful campaign of Agricola, governor of Britain from AD 77 to 84. Perthshire was the northernmost Roman frontier, and occasional forays further north were short-lived.

Having expanded their empire into what is now Scotland, the Romans built and fortified a land frontier which stretched from Ardoch, near present-day Braco, through to Perth. Although they advanced up through Strathmore, and occasionally further north, it was the line of defence through Perthshire known today as the Gask Ridge that appears to have been the most organised and well-defended against possible attack from the north. From the large fort of Ardoch, the defensive line stretched in a north-easterly direction, with smaller forts dotted along the way, eventually arriving at the next larger fort of Strageath, situated just south of the River Earn. Then the line turned east, before turning north towards a fort called 'Bertha', situated on the north side of the confluence of the rivers Almond and Tay. Traces of sections of this Roman road and defence line can just be detected in places, but few of the forts are easy to see. The three largest forts of Ardoch, Strageath and Perth each covered an area of almost 9 acres, with timber buildings filling their interiors, ramparts protected by ditches, and additional housing for non-Roman auxiliary troops who made up the main frontier garrison. Only from the air can the outline of these substantial forts be seen, and it is tantalising only to be able to imagine the bustling day-to-day lifestyle of those Romans so far from home.

Dotted between these large forts were at least 18 watchtowers, many of which are still to be excavated. Each of these timber towers, built nearly 30 feet high on four massive posts, was surrounded by earth ramparts and a ditch, with a single entrance facing the road. There were also turf- and timber-built forts, about 25 m across, of which only three are known today. It is possible to pick out this Roman defence line quite easily on a modern Ordnance Survey map, but much more detail is available with the assistance of a book called *The Romans in Perthshire* by David Woolliscroft and Birgitta Hoffman, from which much of the information here was drawn.

It is telling that the line drawn by the Romans across Perthshire was, centuries later, to become known as 'the Highland Line', marking the staging-post where the drovers with their cattle came down from the north to meet the cattle buyers from the south. The latter refused, probably wisely, to venture further north. The Highlanders had a well-deserved reputation for ferocity, and it became the responsibility of the Black Watch militia to police this frontier. The Black Watch was raised in a unique way. In the wake of the 1715 Jacobite rebellion, companies of trustworthy Highlanders were formed from loyal clans: Campbells, Grants, Frasers, Munros. It was a highly perceptive strategy to gather clans together to cooperate for a common purpose, and over the years, peace descended on the Highlands.

Six companies were formed and stationed in small detachments across the Highlands to prevent fighting between the clans, to deter raiding and to assist in enforcing the laws against the carrying of weapons.

The Black Watch is one of the most famous of the Scottish Regiments, and today its original headquarters in the centre of Perth commemorates the long and illustrious history of the regiment.

The end of the Jacobite rebellions closed a chapter in what might well have developed into a lengthy and bloody civil war in Scotland. After that, local military units sprang up all around Scotland, for national defence rather than for inter-clan warfare. Perthshire contributed its share of small defence forces, such as the Perthshire Fencibles and the Scottish Horse, but neither survives today.

The Perthshire Fencibles was formed in 1798, but not to unanimous acclaim. It was a type of 'Dad's Army', charged with defending the area should Napoleon venture northwards by sailing up the Tay. An Act of Parliament had required the Lords Lieutenant to raise a conscripted force in the local areas. This was not welcomed by the local Blairgowrie people, who felt greatly aggrieved at the prospect of young, fit and healthy male members of the family, often the single and most vital family breadwinners, being purloined into the army. They displayed their displeasure in no uncertain terms when they discovered that the local schoolmaster had acted in an underhand way by offering a list of young men who could be conscripted.

For many in the small Perthshire town, the idea of defending their land from Napoleon must have felt as alien a concept as an attack from outer space. Eventually, the Perthshire Fencibles was made up of 49 men from the Blairgowrie area, 53 from Alyth, 44 from Rattray and 50 from Meigle, with four or five officers in each company and four sergeants, numbering about 250 men all told. Records show that the Commanding Officer was paid 15s 11d per day, while the rank and file received 1s per day. For the latter, this worked out at roughly £18.50 per year, compared with the average lowest grade agricultural worker's wage of £25. It was hardly surprising that the raw conscripts felt hard done by. But the Perthshire Fencibles had at least one reason to be cheerful. They never fought in action, and were disbanded in 1802.

It was almost another century before another military unit was raised in Perthshire – the Scottish Horse. Although not as famous as the Black Watch, and long since lost as a unit in its own right, the Scottish Horse enjoyed a brief, distinguished, history. Their original

Members of the Scottish Horse pose in front of the impressive entrance to Dunkeld House, built as a summer residence for the wife of the 7th Duke of Atholl in 1900. This photo is dated 1939. Today this entrance is well known in Dunkeld as the entrance to Dunkeld House Hotel, and has been under several hotelier owners.

Relaxing after the cessation of the Boer War in 1902, members of the Scottish Horse in a training camp at Blair Atholl inn 1904, applying spit and polish to saddles and bridles.

Drill Hall building still stands at the south side of the Cross in Dunkeld, and until recently was a museum dedicated to the history of the regiment. This proud building still carries the coat of arms above the door, and conveys every impression of being the home base of a very local regiment. However, the raising and formation of the Scottish Horse was not carried out initially in Scotland, as the name might suggest, but thousands of miles away in South Africa where Lord Tullibardine, son of the seventh duke of Atholl, was already writing to his father about the dire condition of the country, and the hatred he and his fellow soldiers had for the Boers. This early correspondence eventually led to the formation of the regiment, but just how this evolved constitutes an intriguing tale.

Tullibardine wrote to his father on 3 December 1899 from Pietermaritzburg where

We are encamped on the race course, having arrived here on the 26th to get our horses fit. Today is one of the hottest days I have ever felt.

Scottish Horse soldiers carry out a training exercise in 1914, practising bridge building over the River Tilt.

Arrived at Eastcourt at about 5am. Horses travelled well, one only being damaged, having fallen down in the open truck which contained 19.

The house next door to the camp is a nice little building with a verandah under which we sit all day. It is all closed up and the garden all in disorder. It is very sad – the owner of it was a well known farmer about 35 years old he has given some valuable information to our troops, and the Boers, thinking him too useful, murdered him as he went out to his farm; he leaves a widow and two children.

We are in under the command of Dundonald.

P.S. You might let some of the people about see this letter or a copy, but not to be published, of course. I have seen many a

Scotchmen here, but none from our part of the world. The tailor's son is at Ladysmith probably, Robertson's (Dunkeld) son is I fancy quite safe. The stationmaster at Durban was on the line at Abercairney, one Duncan, who comes from Kirriemuir.

On 16 December, his birthday, he wrote:

My dear Father,
   I am taking advantage of this short armistice with the Boers to write . . .
   I was once walking up Glen Tilt above Clach Glas when I saw a rabbit come out of a hole on the other side of the river. I was cruel enough to take a long shot at him and I saw him retire to his hole and sit there trying to pick the pellets off. It cured me of taking long shots. Well, yesterday we walked out full of buck and wondering if the Boers would only wait long enough to receive our bayonets; since then we have been sitting picking bullets out back in our camp, having received a first class hiding, and quite cured of making any frontal attack on the Boers.

He continued to describe the enemy's position as 'a huge semi-circle of high hills about as big as Tulloch but much steeper and covered with high boulders . . .'. [Tulloch Hill is adjacent to Blair Atholl.]
   Lord Kitchener, the then Commander of the armed Forces in South Africa, sent a telegram to Tullibardine in November 1900. Kitchener had taken over from Lord Roberts in 1900, in order to gain control of the large area in the Transvaal and what had been the Orange Free State in the continuing Boer War. An offer had been received from the Caledonian Society of Johannesburg to form a corps under the name of the Scottish Horse, and the Society could draw upon the many in the area who were descended from Scots. Tullibardine was at the time a Staff Captain with the First Cavalry Brigade in Natal, and he co-opted two others, Captain Arthur Blair of the King's Own Scottish Borderers and Captain Sir William Dick-Cunyngham of the Black Watch, to help. By February 1901, the Scottish Horse was an entity, four squadrons strong with not only 50 special scouts – necessary, as this was to be mainly guerrilla warfare – but also 50 cyclists. The Scottish theme was marked by the addition of a black grouse cock's tail on their broad felt-brimmed hats.

The battles were well recorded, and logbooks of the day-to-day life of the regiment are still retained in the Dunkeld Cathedral Chapter Archives. One record from 30 October 1901 tells of a Captain Murray who, having been wounded and taken prisoner by the Boers, was stripped of his possessions before being eventually released. His claim for a tunic, puttee leggings, breeches, boots, spurs, watch hat, British Warm coat and Sam Browne belt, as well as a signet ring, valued at £8, and a cigarette case, valued at £1 5s, came to a total of £24. The claim was honoured, with the exception of the ring and cigarette case.

From these beginnings so far from the family homes of Perthshire, the Scottish Horse, although almost disbanded after the end of the Boer War, continued to recruit from Perthshire from then on. Lord Tullibardine proceeded to raise two further regiments, one in Perthshire and the other in north-east Scotland and Argyllshire.

Strong links with Perthshire continued. In 1907 a memorable episode of military manoeuvres took place in the hills between Blairgowrie and Pitlochry, not far from Loch Ordie. Watching were the duke of Connaught and military attachés of many countries, including Germany. Just within the spirit of rivalry, the Scottish Horse and The Lovat Scouts were engaged in an exercise when Tullibardine's personal ghillie, Sergeant Peter Stewart, was heard to issue the order 'Fix bayonets, boys!' as the Lovat Scouts appeared to be coming rather too close. But blood-letting was avoided, and this local gathering of men went to fight in the terrible battles of World War 1.

On 15 February 1940, however, the Scottish Horse was reborn overnight with an altered name: the 79th (Scottish Horse) Medium Regiment. Two months later, on 15 April, it became the 80th (Scottish Horse) Medium Regiment. This followed the final mounted parade held on the Games Ground east of Birnam in December 1939 before they bade farewell to the Regimental home and moved to their new base at Welbeck Abbey in Nottinghamshire.

Following the cessation of World War II, in which the Scottish Horse had served in north-western Europe, Sicily and Italy, the regiment lingered on, but was amalgamated with the Fife and Forfar Yeomanry in 1956. The Dunkeld Drill Hall then became a regimental museum, opened by the tenth duke of Atholl in 1958. In its comparatively short existence the Scottish Horse had been a regiment of cavalry, scouts, infantry, bicyclists, artillery, tanks and armoured cars.

Soon after the creation of the Scottish Horse Regiment, Blair Atholl estate played a key role in extremely secretive trials of an aircraft which was revolutionary in its day.

Its designer, John William Dunne, was a soldier, author and pilot. Inspired by a Jules Verne story at the age of 13, Dunne dreamed of a flying machine that needed no steering and could right itself regardless of wind or weather. Like many other early aircraft designers, he had closely observed not only birds in flight but also the seedhead of *Zanonia Macrocarpa*, which has a half-moon shape. While the shape lent itself readily to gliding, early pioneers had encountered problems when they attempted to add an engine to their tail-less gliders. But Dunne persisted, and produced a design which, though controversial, was the first successful tail-less aircraft. The shape of the plane itself presents an extraordinary image to us today: a squat, foreshortened body with swept-back wings, and its rear end chopped off. But this shape might well have contributed to the eventual design of a helicopter or Harrier jump jet half a century later.

Construction and flight testing of the first Dunne aircraft, the D.1-A, were conducted under great secrecy. The flimsy craft was transported by rail in July 1907 to Blair Atholl, where Dunne carried out one successful eight-second flight with an associate, Colonel Capper, who went along for the ride. Colonel Capper was slightly injured in the crash that terminated the flight, but the experimental glider had demonstrated the stability Dunne that considered so essential. Although the army decided that his glider was not to their advantage, and declined to take it further, Dunne was not one to give up lightly. He continued with more experiments until ill health forced him to give up in 1913, and his new prototype biplane, developed at Blair Atholl so clandestinely, was sold to the Burgess Company in the United States.

Blair Atholl played another surprising role in World War II, as the base for a prisoner-of-war camp at Calvine, one of many in Perthshire.

There were World War I prisoner-of-war camps at Drumbuach Wood by Methven, Little Balbrogie by Ardler and Strathord by Luncarty, but little evidence is left today. Traces of World War II camps, airfields and supply depots are scattered around Perthshire, but the only substantial and well-preserved camp can be seen at

The remains of a blast shelter at Scone Airport, used for protecting vehicles from damage in case of bombs falling.

Cultybraggan at Comrie, while the smaller camp nearby at Dalginross has completely vanished. In 1966, when the camp at Cultybraggan was still in use for cadet training, a thoughtful and perceptive article 'Comrie, Our Village' was published by the local Women's Rural Institute. Did anyone, they pondered, consider the irony in the fact that, almost two millennia before, the Romans had set up a camp at what is now known as Dalginross in Comrie? In a strange reversal of history, many of the prisoners-of-war were of Italian origin and now found themselves under the jurisdiction of Britons, a people whom the Romans from Italy had strived to incorporate into their empire all those centuries ago.

Another camp for Italian prisoners-of-war was based near Alyth, where the inmates were put to work in soft fruit production. Rumour

One of several relics of the wartime use of Scone Airport, a tangled section of metal which lies abandoned in woodland.

had it that the local children spent so much time talking to them that they could speak Italian as well as English by the end of the war.

At Scone, wartime concrete bunkers can just be made out still, directly before the lay-by at Balbeggie farm road. The Scone aerodrome covered a large area, and remained in use for many years as a pilot training school. It is now covered in turf, and World War II ammunition and petrol dumps can still be found.

One example of an RAF airfield which eventually became the site of a key prisoner-of-war camp was at Findo Gask. This is located at Clathymore, about six miles west of Perth, and was in use as an airfield from June 1941 to September 1948, at which point it was used to house German POWs, and named Camp 223.

Today only the three-storey control tower remains to remind

More remains of wartime use. Robust structures built to protect personnel from bombing raids still survive almost camouflaged in the birch trees.

us of the role this area played in World War II, whereas originally there was an operational airfield with three grass runways, offices, accommodation and a pumping station from Pitcarnie Loch, which was used to supply the airfield and camp with water. In addition to the control tower there were numerous blast shelters, an electrical substation and a radio broadcasting house. This airfield appears to have been used as an alternative when other airfields, such as Edzell, were busy. Again it is extraordinary to think that this airfield lies within a mile or so of one of the major Roman camps.

The Strathallan Aircraft Collection was an ambitious attempt by Sir William Roberts, the owner of Strathallan Castle near Auchterarder, to assemble a large collection of old aircraft, in effect saving many from the scrapheap or from being left to rot. In purchasing these

The semi-derelict control tower for Clathymore, a World War II airfield which then became a prisoner-of-war camp. Now surrounded by new houses, the control tower is being renovated as a house.

historic aircraft he not only preserved them, he also aimed to restore them to airworthy condition, frequently re-building them as required. Although he had commenced his collection when living in the south of England, he brought it to Strathallan in 1971, running air shows and attracting enthusiasts to view such aircraft as a Fairey Swordfish, a Fairey Battle, the Rolls Royce 'Flying Bedstead' (forerunner of the Harrier jump jet), a Lancaster bomber, and a Spitfire. By the time the collection had to be dispersed in 1980, the Perthshire skies had been filled with the nostalgic hum of many of these elderly aircraft flying overhead.

But Perthshire may well have been echoing to the sounds of other enemy planes or tanks if events had taken a different turn in 1940. In a desolate area of Glenshee are concrete blocks, still visible on the south side of the summit of the A93, related to a significant date in British wartime history.

Dr Gordon Barclay explained much of the planning and construction of this defence line in his detailed study; *The Cowie Line: A Second World War Stop-line West of Stonehaven, Aberdeenshire* (Edinburgh, Society of Antiquaries of Scotland, 2005).

On 7 September 1940, the wartime 51st Division issued Operational Instruction No 1, relating to in the event of an invasion. These instructions were to be carried out if the code word 'Cromwell' came down the line. Although this warning was only to Southern and Eastern Commands in England, and supposedly copied in to other commands, the warning was taken seriously enough in the Scottish Command for the church bells to be sounded in Stonehaven. Fortunately, it was to prove a false alarm.

With the passage of time, it is difficult to imagine the stark terror of an imminent invasion in 1940. The south-east coast of England was the most likely area where enemy troops would land, but the code word 'Cromwell' applied not only to the south-east of England but also to an area stretching for 400 miles to the north, to the coastline round by Kincardineshire and Aberdeenshire. It was directly related to a significant event not far from the Scottish coast.

The fall of Norway on 3 May 1940, which placed Nazi troops and air power much closer to the north-east of Scotland, was perceived as an immensely dangerous threat. On 10 May, there was a meeting of the Home Defence Executive. The idea was simple: to stop an invading enemy pushing inland if they landed on the beaches. While many of these long stretches of beaches were also backed by steep cliffs, for example at St Cyrus in Kincardineshire, many other beaches, especially those north of Aberdeen, simply sloped gently into farmland, and the great open areas would have been all too easy for the deployment of tanks. The area of north-east Scotland was in the charge of General Ironside, who summed up the forces at his disposal as 'not only ill-equipped; they also lacked mobility.' Clearly, if an invasion force arrived, he knew how vulnerable the area's defences would be. So he made his highest priority not only the construction of a defensive line, known as a 'coastal crust', to delay any invading army, but also a second line of defence if the invaders pressed inland. At best, it was hoped that delaying tactics would be effective. The commanders knew full well that they had far too few men on the ground to completely stop a powerful line of enemy tanks.

In the north-east this defensive line became known as 'the Cowie Line', after the Cowie Water which flows due east until its outfall into the sea at Stonehaven. This was perceived as one of the most likely routes to be taken by an invading army, and the construction of an anti-tank stop line, known as a Command Line, was set in motion by

The double bends of the Devil's Elbow road are negotiated by the royal car containing Queen Elizabeth II and the Duke of Edinburgh in the 1950s. Clearly visible are the concrete blocks of the Cowie Line defences, constructed during the 1940s.

Scottish Command. This ran from Dysart in Fife to Loch Tummel in Perthshire. The line was composed of an anti-tank barrier, including anti-tank walls, adapted rail embankments, pillboxes (concrete lookout shelters with windows all round) and anti-tank cubes. These latter were square blocks of concrete put in place in order to impede the advance of tanks. Some contained square holes through which a steel girder could have been inserted, to strengthen the block and, hopefully, further impede an advancing tank.

It was a substantial area for ill-equipped and scattered troops to protect from advancing enemy tanks, so their role was to interfere with and delay landing, to cover communication for reinforcements and to effect static defence of vulnerable points such as aerodromes and ports. It was conceded by Basil Collier in *The Defence of the United Kingdom*, published by Her Majesty's Stationery Office in 1957, that 'The degree of resistance of such detachments must be to the last man'. Even today this resonates clearly as a doom-laden scenario.

Every effort was made to impede the progress of tanks. Several bridges were identified for demolition, rows of five-foot-high concrete cubes were put in place to impede tanks and lines of ditches five-feet deep were dug, taking care not to bank the removed soil up more than two feet high so as not to provide cover to enemy gunners. The pillboxes had to be bulletproof, and later design specifications required the walls to be built of reinforced concrete 3 feet 6 inches thick and the roofs to be 12 inches thick.

Today, it is possible to see remnants of these anti-tank boxes at Glenshee. Only one pillbox and about half the anti-tank cubes survive. Since the 1950s the road has been continuously improved, and the notorious double bend of the old 'Devil's Elbow' was finally swept away in the 1960s. The double bend had stymied many a motorist and led to the frequent closure of the road during snowy winters, as most cars would stall or slide. So it is humbling to reflect on just how, in the midst of war, in a remote area and with the added hazard of single track, sharply bending roads, the transport of the materials for such substantial constructions and then the construction itself were achieved in a few months.

The defensive line at Glenshee, which was always referred to as a section of the Cowie Line, would prevent enemy advances into Moray, Aberdeen and Perthshire.

Thankfully an invasion never took place, but enough of the Cowie Line survives to give an indication of a vital line of defence.

Not only defence was uppermost in the minds of the government as war became a reality. Perthshire mansions and hospitals were converted to accommodate the expected intake of war wounded, but even before these measures were put in place in the mid-twentieth century, various spas around the county were offering their own solutions to ill health.

Perthshire produced its fair share of medical practitioners from the seventeenth century onwards. Some would study to be surgeons in a nearby town. For example, in 1753 William Wright left his home town of Crieff at the age of seventeen to serve his apprenticeship as a surgeon in Falkirk. Others began their careers as gardeners, advancing to the early botanic gardens in Edinburgh or Glasgow, both of which had established physic gardens in the very early 1700s. The monks of the monasteries at Dunkeld, Coupar Angus and Dunblane, as well as Perth, would have cultivated their physic gardens as a rich source of health-giving herbs. Many local Perthshire doctors, as well as the many purveyors of doubtful medical remedies, appear in the early tales of Perthshire.

In the seventeenth and eighteenth centuries, goats were not only useful for their wool and meat, their milk was widely believed to possess curative powers over human ailments. The practice might well have been widespread, although there is little evidence to support this, but the belief that goats milk enhanced good health was taken up with alacrity by several ministers of the church in the 1740s. These were no ordinary, established men of the cloth, and their visit to Logie Almond to partake of goat's milk for the good of their health also had another purpose. Nicknamed the 'First Mighties', these four ministers from in and around Perth were one of the breakaway groups from the established Church of Scotland. David Marshall Forrester wrote in his 1844 book on Perthshire that,

> The goats were brought down to Kipney, and milked at the road going west between the two woods short of the Lodge Gate, while the waters of Lag-na-chian spring were also sought after. . . . Ministers who came for rest and change and bracing air and drinking of the goat's milk were wont to preach to the people, not in church or chapel or hall, for of those there was none, but on the braes or in the Den in the open air.

No such preaching took place at another health-giving spot. Although Pitkeathly Wells spent its final days storing Schweppes tonic water, this curious little rounded house, which sits on a right-angled bend on a side road just a couple of miles west of Bridge of Earn, had enjoyed for hundreds of years a reputation for healing, as one of the many spas in Scotland, and one of the very few in Perthshire.

No one is quite sure how the water at the Pitkeathly spring was found to be beneficial. William Marshall, writing in 1881 in *Historic Scenes of Perthshire*, suggested two possible reasons: firstly, that in the Middle Ages the locals had noticed pigeons drinking the waters and had followed suit; or, secondly, that reapers had found that the waters quenched their thirst at midday from throats dry and irritated with chaff and dust. But by 1771 the watering-hole had disintegrated into a disreputable place. The popularity of the wells came to the attention of the Kirk Session of Dunbarney, who took immediate steps to bring order to proceedings, at least on the Sabbath. Annoyed by the 'desecration committed by crowds who visited the wells on the Holy day', whom they darkly suspected as coming from the 'Fair City of Perth', they issued orders which would effectively stop much of the crowd in its tracks. They decreed that the boatman at Dunbarney, John Vallance, was to be forbidden to give them passage. They even decreed further stern measures, if necessary, for the folk to be stopped by constables with the authority of the Justices of the Peace.

John Grant, a former Chief Justice in Jamaica, acquired the Pitkeathly estates in 1793. Within a year he was receiving complaints about the pollution of the healing wells, by the 'leaving of distempered limbs therein'. It all began to sound more than disreputable, even a danger to health. Clearly, he had not bought the wells in order to obtain a malodorous problem. He turned the predicament over in his mind. Being a man of some spirit, and seeing a development opportunity, he decided to turn the wells into a spa. From then on the wells climbed sharply up the social order, and as a spa, Pitkeathly was relaunched to the more genteel classes. It was probably Grant who installed the first pump to ensure a supply of clean water, and a bath house where water would be dispensed and hot baths furnished.

Word spread that Pitkeathly Wells had become a clean and pleasant place to visit, and they took on a much wider popularity, attracting interest from much further afield. In 1814, Dr William Horsley published an exhaustive treatise on the components of the waters as well as their benefits. He discussed at length the benefits of drinking the water with rhubarb, Epsom salts, or Jamaican ginger, as well as with whisky, and the various advantages of bathing parts of the body in the water, or indeed total submersion. He waxed eloquent in his praise of the trip to the wells from Perth's Salutation Inn, which no doubt added greatly to the trade of the inn, the wells and the local stagecoach. All of this can have done little to help the men he was employed to care for, those being several thousand French prisoners of war under the guard of the Durham Regiment, of which Dr Horsley was the Medical Officer.

Pitkeathly Wells was the popular spa just south of Perth and close to Bridge of Earn, and enjoyed two centuries of popularity.

The wells flourished and became a local meeting place with a reputation for fostering romance. The ballad of 'Pitkeathly Wells' was reputed to be directed to one Jeannie Oliphant by the Earl of Kinnoull. Sadly, she turned her attentions elsewhere and wed another.

In 1859, a pavilion had been built where spa-water was sold over the counter, and in 1886, a report revealed how the pavilion was enhanced by the addition of a veranda, a private room just for ladies, a smoking room just for gentlemen, and a reading room with newspapers, periodicals and a piano. There were grounds where one could play bowls, croquet or tennis and the church had clearly decided to join in the cause. A Free Kirk minister, named appropriately Mr Wells, preached to crowds of over 200 on Sunday evenings.

Leslie's Directory for Perthshire, in 1892, advertised 'Pitkeathly, Prince of Table Waters, sole Proprietors Reid and Donald of Perth. His Grace, the Duke of Atholl, KT has kindly given us permission to attest that the Soda, Potash, Seltzer and Pitkeathly waters supplied by us to Blair Castle for the last ten years have given entire satisfaction. Blair Castle 29 May 1890. To be had of all chemists and Mineral Water Dealers and at the Principal Hotels.'

About twenty years later, the decline in popularity of spas was evident as belief in the healing power of such water waned. The Pitkeathly Wells were leased to the Schweppes Company who carried on the tradition of selling water in the pavilion, although tea on the lawn or the veranda was proving much more popular. During World War I attitudes changed. Schweppes expanded the manufacturing side for their tonic waters, employing thirty staff. However, that enterprise ended in 1927 when a fire destroyed the machinery. From then until the end of the century, the spa buildings were used by Schweppes for storage. It is now a private house.

The growth of the village of Bridge of Earn in the nineteenth century was linked to the popularity of nearby Pitkeathly Wells, which ceased to function as a spa in 1949. The area, though, continued to be closely associated with health, but developed as a hospital, with medical treatment based on established scientific facts, rather than the questionable benefits of Pitkeathly's spa water. Across the eastern side of the village, a sprawling set of single-storey prefabricated buildings had sprung up, housing a hospital. Bridge of Earn Hospital was one of Perthshire's principal medical centres and a major source of employment until it was closed in 1993. Transferred to the National Health Service in 1948, the hospital was built on a farm named Oudenarde, after one of the Duke of Marlborough's victories in 1708. It is now demolished.

The enormous casualty lists of World War I were still a vivid memory when plans for building large numbers of temporary hospitals were drawn up in 1939. These structures were built with impressive speed to a standard design, strategically sited at a distance from industrial areas but close to the railway network. Bridge of Earn hospital opened in 1940 with space for 1,020 patients. The earliest admissions were mainly from neighbouring military camps, patients with tuberculosis, and prisoners of war. The busiest time for the hospital came in 1944, initially with casualties of the V1 and V2 bombing of London, and then the Normandy invasion.

'We were full after D-Day,' recalled one Sister. 'They always came during the night, often treated, but with their first field dressings still in place. From time to time a convoy of German POWs arrived, and their wounds were horrific – they had not had access to penicillin.' By 1945 there were 1,280 patients, with convoys arriving every weekend. Specially adapted hospital trains arrived at Perth station bringing large numbers of wounded servicemen who were then transferred to fleets of ambulance wagons and taken to Bridge of Earn Hospital. One former ambulance driver later remembered, 'Once you had your four patients you had to follow the very faint light of the ambulance in front – a slow process as your lights were only slits cut across normal lights painted black. At Bridge of Earn Hospital we delivered the wounded and went to another ward for blankets for our next contingent. The lovely cups of tea given by WVS mobile canteens at the station were very welcome.'

As happened during World War I, many large houses and hotels were also requisitioned and modified for medical and convalescent use. Beds replaced antique furniture in grand drawing rooms. Dupplin Castle, near Forteviot, and Taymouth Castle at Kenmore were two, while the Murthly Asylum Hospital was also used. The magnificent building of Dupplin was demolished in 1967, and the central building of the Murthly hospital has vanished recently.

At the Gleneagles Hotel, the era of partying, dining and socialising gave way to more serious business as it was also transformed into a military hospital. The hotel's finery was placed in storage and the golf course bunkers filled in to avoid enemy detection. The bridal suite was converted into operating theatres, the lights for these being provided by spotlights from Henry Hall's orchestra. The first convoy of 191 patients from the battle of Narvik in Norway arrived in May 1940, and many more followed from Dunkirk. Famous patients who were treated included film stars Stewart Granger and David Niven. Later in the war, the hospital became a fitness centre for Scottish miners. The German Foreign Minister von Ribbentrop had stayed at Gleneagles before the war, and apparently had it in mind as a private residence after the Nazi victory.

While the mansion houses of Dupplin and Taymouth were transformed into hospitals to nurse wounded soldiers returning from

The entrance to Taymouth Castle from the model village of Kenmore with the Reading Room to the left of the picture reflect an era of paternalism and high spending which evaporated in the 20th century.

both world wars, buildings as substantial, but purpose-built, had also sprung up to treat that most pernicious of diseases before the availability of modern medicines: tuberculosis.

The Ochil Hills Hospital was built as a TB sanatorium in 1902 on the upper slopes of the eastern Ochils, to the northwest of Milnathort. Tucked away up a mile-long track and with spectacular views to the south, its isolated location was perfect for the treatment popular at the time. Patients would be encouraged to sleep or be outside in the fresh air as much as possible. The Ochil Hills Hospital ceased to be used in the late 1980s, and the main hospital building and associated annexe buildings were demolished in 2003.

Visitors to Taymouth Castle could be charmed by the extravagance of the decorated ceilings in the main rooms of the castle, such as this one mingling fanciful knights jousting, and vivid colouring. Hospital patients occupied this castle during World War II, and would have gazed up at this ceiling.

Out of the way as many patients must have felt at the Ochil Hills Hospital, it was but a half hour's car journey from Perth. For those in Corrour Old Lodge, 1,723 feet above sea level. there was even more extreme isolation. Access was over the hill from Loch Rannoch, by means of the old drovers' road to the west. The Lodge had once enjoyed the status of Scotland's highest shooting lodge. The railway that opened in 1894 led to replacement of the original building by a more easily accessible lodge at the east end of Loch Ossian in 1897. The Old Lodge then became an isolation hospital for a few years but was de-roofed in the 1930s.

No more isolated place can be imagined. The Youth Hostel at Loch Ossian is the former boathouse for the small ferry that took guests up to the new shooting lodge. For an ill patient to have finished the journey by boat must have felt like reaching the end of the world.

CHAPTER 3

THE HARNESSING OF THE GREAT RIVERS OF PERTHSHIRE

Water was the life-blood and powerhouse of Perthshire. The many lochs and the rivers Earn, Almond and Tay offered a means of transport and produced fish in abundance, and their tributaries were harnessed to drive many of the mills which thrived in the eighteenth and nineteenth centuries, while the fabric-weaving mills at Stanley and Luncarty even survived until the 1980s.

Being close to a mill lade was an early version of being plugged into the main electricity grid. Water powered the machinery necessary for the success of several substantial businesses in Perthshire. Although little remains of the thriving bleach-fields of Luncarty, the names of two of Perthshire's most eminent self-made men from the textiles business are still remembered: Sandeman and Marshall.

William Sandeman was the original patron of the library in Perth, while Thomas Hay Marshall is remembered for funding the Museum and Art Gallery and his name still adorns the portico. Sandeman was born in the Alyth area in 1722, and belonged to a 'confusingly prolific family', according to Anthony Cooke, in his *History of Redgorten Parish*. Sandeman was clearly a person of great determination and application from a young age, and was appointed as a stamp master of linen and hemp on 13 June 1746, when he would have been merely 23 years old. This appointment was made by the Board of Trustees for Manufacturers, a government body, and after four years of his 'diligent work' he was given a bonus of £25 as a reward. Sandeman had positioned himself perfectly to become the trusted middleman between the Board and the manufacturers. Accordingly, the Board turned to him in the 1750s when they sought to effect expert improvements in the linen industry, and to organise the distribution of spinning and reeling machinery, and flax. But the time also appeared ripe for him to set himself up as a businessman, using his wide-ranging knowledge for his own gain.

In 1752, he laid out a bleach-field at Luncarty, on a bog known as the 'Myretoun of Luncarty'. Having raised £1,300, he spent this on levelling the twelve acres of ground, and constructing flat bleaching areas and buildings. At a time when a farm labourer earned around £17 a year, a skilled textile worker £34, and even a professional managerial engineer only £137, this was an enormous sum to raise. Perhaps some came from his family, but one imagines that banks and investors both would have been willing to invest in someone with significant and proven expertise. He then proceeded to transform the area into 'lawns, orchards, grass parks, cornfields and bleaching greens', and built 'a commodious village' for the essential workforce. In order to make the most of his new arrangement and reduce the risk of flooding, he had a new channel dug for the course of both the Ordie and Shochie Burns, converting this into a 'neat canal' for the bleach fields.

The importance of bleach-fields was paramount. Housewives could maintain the snowy appearance of their linen by spreading it out, often coated with soap, on grassy areas to bleach in the sun or frost. Bleaching the massive amounts of white cotton and linen used in every household until the 1950s was part and parcel of life. But behind the highly desirable whiteness of linen and cotton lay a process which required acres of ground, and foul-smelling toxic procedures.

The only successful method of bleaching in the 1750s, when Sandeman established his business, was to steep the cloth in a hot alkaline solution, 'the ley', then to wash it out, dry it and apply an acid, 'the sour', until the cloth changed from a grubby, uneven brown to as close to a pure white as possible. Ashes were used to make the leys until the introduction of chlorine in the late 1780s, and from the late 1740s sulphuric acid replaced traditional bran or sour buttermilk. The cloth remained pegged out, undergoing this slow process, for five to eight weeks at a time. Sandeman also built a drying house, and a 'Water mill for Washing and Rubbing Cloth after the Irish method'. This appeared to accelerate the process. His business verve and application of new methods meant that not only did he manage to bring the method of bleaching to the highest standard, he also reduced the price by a penny a yard.

His venture proved greatly successful. In 1761 he claimed to have spent a further £2,486 on laying out the bleach-fields and £1,030 on

Linen bleaching and drying on the North Inch was guarded by Bob Sidey, who could take refuge inside his portable shed, with attached dog kennel.

improvements. He employed, perhaps poached, skilled workmen from the British Linen Company's bleach-field at Saltoun in East Lothian, and one Hector Turnbull, the son of a Berwickshire farmer, not only became a foreman and then partner in the business, but in the meantime married into the Sandeman family.

Praise was heaped on Sandeman. He was lauded for the care he gave to his workforce, including building sturdy housing for them, and he continued to expand. He visited Richard Arkwright, the pioneer of water-powered cotton spinning to learn about cotton production, and he solved the problem of water shortages in the summer months by digging a canal two miles long from the River Tay to the bleach-fields, at one point cutting through solid rock. By the time of his death in 1790 he left behind a considerable business empire, and had founded a dynasty. His grandson, another William Sandeman, drove the business forward, expanding the bleach-fields to cover some 80 acres.

He had been a paternalistic employer, and probably a just employer for his day. He was a staunch member of the Glasite Church, as were other prominent business figures in Perthshire, and according to the *Old Statistical Account*, published in the 1790s, his workers were distinguishable by their appearance, the 'cleanliness and neatness of their dress', the 'sprightliness and vivacity in their manner' and their 'gaiety and order which is seldom found in other places'. One wonders if the author was being objective or if he, too, was a member of the Glasite church who were noted for their strict morals. The founder of this church, John Glas, had broken away from the traditions of the established Church of Scotland, as the basis of his theology was that he would under no circumstances accept the control in any form of state over church. The government of the Glasite church was much more democratic. Anyone could offer his thoughts on a theological subject, whatever his background or education. Sandeman workers were severely frowned upon for 'unseemly behaviour', and were strongly encouraged to wed, with the incentive of being provided with married accommodation

With abundant supplies of water from the rivers Almond and Tay, the area supported several cotton mills, and it was a boom time for production. The mills at Stanley were famous for their innovative engineering pioneered by Richard Arkwright, whose forward-thinking creation of water-powered mills increased production dramatically, and a Stanley mill stands sentinel today to the quality of his construction. Another thriving mill was sited at the quaintly named Cromwellpark, close to present-day Pitcairngreen.

Cromwellpark had nothing to do with Cromwell or the Civil War, but was a derivation of the old Scots name of Cromwell Craigs – 'craigs' being a 'high hill'. The area is characterised by a series of terraced slopes going down to the flat areas by the River Almond. The mill, established there in 1782 by William Macalpine, was initially set up as a print-works for textiles.

The huge companies were but one aspect of weaving in Perthshire. For many weaving had been an extra, but essential, part of the family income, undertaken in the family home. Throughout Perthshire there were villages and hamlets filled with self-employed weavers, all working away in their homes. This home industry reached its zenith in the late 1700s and early 1800s, when machinery and industrialisation began to gain momentum.

But black days lurked just round the corner. A far-off disaster

One side of an outflow lade from a mill connected to the Luncarty bleachfields.

triggered one of the most spectacular financial crashes affecting the entire textile industry, and changing the history of Perthshire.

The wars with France, according to G. Penny's 1836 edition of *Traditions of Perth*, reduced trade to 'more of the hazardous character of gambling than of fair trade'. But it was a fire in Spain which brought catastrophe. In 1810, the textile businesses in Perth were undergoing spectacular rises and falls, and bankruptcies. But these ups and downs were nothing compared with the fire which wiped out £100,000 worth of goods which had been sent from the Cromwellpark company, via their London branch, to Cadiz in Spain. The goods were lost, with no compensation. The loss bankrupted the company, and brought down 60 other dependent, small textile manufacturers in Perthshire. The larger companies, such as at Stanley, simply closed

Still in remarkable condition, the other side of the outflow lade (see previous page) was to supply a mill wheel outflow, with a lock control supplying the water.

down in 1814 for nine years. The Luncarty bleach-fields survived on a reduced scale, after boardroom battles which bankrupted two of the company directors involved, William Turnbull and John Sandeman. The company survived, with new directors.

By 1837 the Luncarty bleach-fields employed fewer than half the 300 workers they had employed in 1795, but it was now so highly mechanised that they could bleach two million yards of linen cloth, compared with 500,000 to 600,000 yards forty years earlier. The mechanisation consisted of 28 sets of beetling machines for finishing the cloth by pounding it, with a corresponding number of calenders, washing stocks, and running boards. The cloth was dried using steam-heated cylinders. As mechanisation increased, so the workforce dwindled.

The Marshalls retained control of the business until 1900, then control passed to a group of trustees, and the company was finally bought in 1917 by the Manchester-based Bleachers Association for £120,000. Due to the scarcity of linen at the end of World War I, cotton became the mainstay of the business, but by the late 1920s high demand from the leisure sector in the United States put fine linen production back on top.

Luncarty was described as a model village, with 120 houses for its 350 employees. While the original William Sandeman might well have been a paternalistic employer for his day in providing good quality accommodation, the effect of this 'tied house' – housing available only for the company workers – was to favour the owner more than the worker. Workers were tied to their jobs by the occupancy of their house, and vice versa. George Miller, born in Luncarty in 1900, was one of five members of his family, and several generations, to work in the bleach-fields. His memories of the early days of living in the 'model village' were less than rosy.

George was 14 when he started work at the outbreak of World War I, and was employed to operate a calender, a job he hated. A calender was a press with two rollers, akin to a mangle, for smoothing the cloth, a very monotonous task, and it required constant feeding. Young George worked a 12-hour day from 6 a.m. to 6 p.m. with two hours off, one for breakfast at 9 a.m. and another for lunch at one o'clock. Although the sight of thousands of yards of cloth pegged out in the fields to bleach for weeks was over by the time he joined, and the bleaching was done by chemicals, he recalled that the industry was still a large employer. By the end of the war, 400 people worked in the Luncarty Mill, and much mechanisation was taking place. It was a far cry from the day his great-grandfather transported cloth from Dunfermline to Luncarty by horse and cart in 1869. Conditions in the tied houses, too, were far from efficient or comfortable. Advanced though many of the houses might have been when they were first built, by the early part of the twentieth century, they were distressingly poor.

'The sanitation was terrible,' remembered George. 'The toilets were just pails, and twice a week a cart came round to empty them. The cart then emptied at the end of a field which was overrun by rats. Water was carried into the houses by buckets which were drawn by hand pumps. The parish school was at Redgorton, a good mile from the village. When I went to school in 1905 we had a headmaster and lady teacher. We started, I think at 9 a.m. and from then until the end of the school day at 4 p.m. I had just a jelly piece for dinner.'

The remnants of the Luncarty bleach-field works only vanished at the end of the twentieth century, and until their final days, production existed in a Dickensian sprawl of brick and iron sheds, criss-crossed by dank, brick canals, with steam pumping out into the surrounding countryside, and a paltry workforce. The actual workspace was eroding year on year as more and more of the buildings became unusable. What is astonishing is that the entire bleaching works had been established in the area in 1752, a span of almost 250 years. In later years, the production of fine damasks and linens from the Perthshire area was principally for hotels, steamship companies, the railway companies and the United States market. No doubt, in many a drawer in Perthshire lurks a matching set of tablecloth and napkins bleached and dyed in one of these Perthshire firms.

But the decline of the big mill companies gathered pace. The American Civil War put paid to many mills spinning cotton, as the raw material was effectively blocked from leaving the southern states. Blairgowrie supported eleven mills in its heyday, but not a single one remains working today, although many of the mill buildings have been adapted for use as housing or small businesses.

Desperation was a frequent occurrence in all the mills, as more and more difficulties appeared. Stanley Mills, for example, were the only ones in the world to have adapted to the manufacturing of cigarette papers in the 1960s and 1970s, selling to Wills and Players. But it was all in vain. Not one of these great old mills, which supported so many employees and churned out miles of cloth by harnessing water as power, still exists today.

Water had also been the source of energy in more rural areas for other, less ambitious mills. In his book *Water Power in Scotland 1550–1870*, John Shaw writes about the different types of mills which sprang up between the end of the eighteenth century and the mid-nineteenth century. Spindle mills were common in Perthshire. The spindles were made from soft wood, such as birch, and, unlikely as it sounds, were shipped from rural Perthshire to the spinning mills of India. Often they would have a ready market locally as well, for example at Trochry near Dunkeld, where the spindles would have been an essential component of the local woollen mill. The jute trade between Dundee and India thrived for most of the nineteenth century, but its demise put paid to the spindle mills.

Two other types of mills reflected the agriculture of the area, and demonstrated strong entrepreneurial traits. Bone mills, for the grinding up of bones for fertiliser, provided a vital source of phosphates. Bone meal mills were initially a novelty, but soon began showing healthy profits, which no doubt encouraged small-scale millers. In 1828 a steam-powered bone mill in Dundee was still sufficiently novel for the Highland Agricultural Society to carry a report on it in its *Transactions*. Between 1830 and 1870, bone mills were set up at a number of sites, close the east coast where bones were imported from Prussia, Russia and the Mediterranean. Later, whale bones were usefully sold by ship owners, but it was considered that animal bones produced the best meal. Around five of these small-scale bone mills existed in Perthshire, using locally-sourced bones.

The success and advancement of farming methods in the rural areas of Perthshire led to by-products emerging, not only from bones, but from another surprising raw ingredient: potatoes.

A third of Scotland's potato, or to use the common Scottish word 'tattie', mills, were clustered in Perthshire – an indication of just how enthusiastically Perthshire grasped the opportunity to add profit to its productive potato crops – for the production of farina, or starch. Some potato mills were adapted from existing mills, such as the corn and flour mill at Coupar Grange, a mile from Coupar Angus. Others appeared to be purpose-built. The starch powder had two main uses. Firstly, it was used to keep the warp threads damp and malleable during the weaving process for both linen and cotton. Secondly, the starch was then regularly used within the large mansion houses to produce very crisp household linen and clothing.

Perhaps one of the first potato mills to be established was situated just below the old meal mill or the 'Muilin Dhu' high up above the hamlet of Tulliemet. It employed around six people. The combination of surplus potatoes and thriving linen industries, including the small-scale weavers in crofts and villages, meant that there was a ready local market for the farina, produced from the potatoes, and further afield, but still within 15 miles, were the large-scale weaving factories at Luncarty and Stanley.

In the nineteenth century, the Tulliemet mill was rebuilt alongside a burn at Kindallachan. It absorbed local crops of potatoes, and

A travelling salesman, typically to be seen on the road until the mid 20th century, may well have carried textiles spun, bleached and dyed in Perthshire.

how this was turned into starch is recorded in the *Third Statistical Account* (1951–52):

> This mill took over surplus potatoes, ground them up and allowed the pulp to settle in large tanks fed from the Tulliemet burn. After settling, the pulp was sluiced away into the burn, leaving the starch or farina, as it was called, to be dried and sold. At times, the waste collected in the pools in the burn when the water was low, made its

presence noticeable owing to the stench created, but the local folk did not seem to notice anything wrong, and it was only visitors who made any comment. In later years the mill was put out of service and the ground floor was used as a recreational hall.

These farine mills in Perthshire were small and, in production, were nothing approaching the size of the steam-powered starch mills in the Paisley area, a zone of spinning and weaving on a massive scale. John Shaw, writing in his book *Water Power in Scotland 1550–1870* observed that in constrast to the production in Perthshire, the production in Paisley was on a massive scale. In order to produce starch at these Paisley mills, they consumed several thousand tons of imported maize, sago and rice, employed 200 workers as well as a steam horse-powered engine.

The power of water rushing down from the hills high above the Tay offered many more opportunities.

Rotmell Farm, three miles to the north of Dunkeld on the Old Military Road running parallel to the A9, is probably one of Perthshire's most imposing farm buildings. Its grandiose scale and commanding position are clearly visible from the B898 which follows the south side of the Tay.

Its elevated position is understandable – close by is the site of an ancient fort, possibly even a castle-type structure. Rotmell, or Rathmell means 'the fort on the hill', and apparently a castle was built on the footprint of an earlier fortification, occupied by Robert II (1371–70) and Robert III (1390–1406), both of whom had been earls of Atholl.

This collection of buildings is a prime example of a 'ferm toun', a farm with many of the employees living in close proximity in a cluster of dwellings, in many ways a village in miniature. The ferm toun at Rotmell comprised about 20 men, some of whom were paid in kind, such as the hill shepherd. He lived close by in Roar Lodge and kept two cows for milk and cheese, and supplemented the family income by selling on any calves. He also kept a pig, and his wages were paid in part by sacks of flour, oatmeal and four tons of coal a year. The farm had its own smiddy, a blacksmith coming over for two to three weeks a year to carry out all the necessary work.

In 1792, when it was the property of the duke of Atholl, the rental was just over £100 per annum, nearly £10,000 in today's money. Built

The Falls of Dochart at Killin were a popular attraction as well as illustrating the power and abundance of water in Perthshire, which led to the creation of the massive hydroelectric schemes in the area.

by the duke in the 1790s as one of three model farm 'villages', this was clearly a thriving establishment. A decade later, the farm's name was changed to St Columba's, later shortened to St Colme's.

In keeping with the fairly flamboyant structure of the farm buildings, a 'Great Wheel' was erected in 1856. This wheel, 22 feet (6.6 metres) in diameter and 3 feet (0.9 metre) wide was constructed of cast and wrought iron, with buckets for scooping up the water. This monster was destined for suitably heavy duties. Operating, for example, as a thrashing mill and bone crusher, it required to be fed with a substantial amount of water. A generous supply, therefore, had to be readily available, and a large mill pond, the remains of which can still be seen, was dug and kept filled behind the farm. Such was

Charles McIntosh, the postman and naturalist who was befriended by Beatrix Potter, stands to the right of the mill gates of the Inver Mill, talking to the lockkeeper.

the importance of the farm at St Colme's, or Rotmell, and the scale of the Great Wheel, that Queen Victoria detoured to go past it on one of her trips to the area in the 1860s.

The wheel and the smiddy survived for almost a century after Queen Victoria's visit. St Colme's had been a special place for the then duchess of Atholl, whom the queen visited in the 1860s. Anne, dowager duchess and widow of the sixth duke, kept her prize Ayrshire herd there. By then, the duchess lived in the Dower House in Dunkeld, but, as Queen Victoria noted in her diary, 'We took tea in the farmhouse, where the Duchess has kept one side to herself, and there she intends to live sometimes with Mrs MacGregor, almost by themselves. From here we drove back and stopped at the byres, closer by the stables, which were lit up with gas, and where we saw all the cows being milked. Very fine Ayrshire cows, and nice dairymaids.'

When the duchess died in 1897, the farm name reverted to Rotmell.

There is a watery endnote to the story of utilising the power of water as transport in Perthshire in the nineteenth century. This was the canal that never was. In 1806 an ambitious project for a canal was surveyed by a highly experienced engineer, Sir John Rennie. Rennie, a farmer's younger son, was born at Phantassie, near East Linton, East Lothian. He demonstrated a taste for mechanics at a very early age, and was allowed to spend much time in the workshop of Andrew Meikle, millwright, the inventor of the threshing machine, who lived at Houston Mill on the Phantassie estate. Inspired by such a background, Rennie made rapid advancement and became an engineer of bridges, noted for the solidity and attention to detail he gave to every project. One of his well known practices was to pay personal visits to possible sites all over the country, in order to make his own detailed measurements of the land and water. His Perthshire remit was simple. He was to produce plans for a canal to link Loch Earn to Perth to carry goods more easily than by track with horse-drawn vehicles. With his known attention to detail, he would most probably have undertaken the surveying himself.

It is very likely that he journeyed to Loch Earn in 1805. Just south of Methven was a large boggy area, known today at Methven Moss. The canal was to be 8 feet deep and 15 feet broad, and was to terminate in the inner harbour in Perth designed by Robert Louis Stevenson's grandfather. This inner harbour was adjacent to the western bank of the river Tay at the South Inch in Perth.

Although many of his projects were south of the Border, Rennie's expertise was so much in demand that he also had advised on the construction of the Glasgow, Paisley and Johnstone Canal, the Forth and Clyde Canal, and the Edinburgh and Glasgow Union Canal extensions. In 1818 he was asked to review the proposals made by Robert Whitworth and Robert Stevenson about a possible link between Arbroath and Forfar. While he expressed doubts about the financial benefits of any canal to Forfar, he did suggest that the line might extend west along the Vale of Strathmore. The route once surveyed by Rennie was eventually used for a railway. The Perth to Crieff railway opened in 1858, and closed in 1965. On modern maps it is possible to follow easily the route of the railway, and imagine a canal alongside.

Water power, though, was ever a useful commodity in Perthshire, and the concept of using such a ready resource has never ceased over the centuries, but nothing in Perthshire's history matched the ambition of the hydroelectric power schemes of the late 1940s and 1950s. These years saw some enormous changes to the Perthshire landscape as hundreds of workmen settled in the areas selected for dam construction. The 'Hydro boys' had arrived and their camps of tin huts, wooden cabins and caravans sprang up in the most rural locations.

As the great dams rose along various Perthshire glens, much of the activity took place out of the sight of the local population. A large international gathering – Scots, Irish, Poles, Germans, prisoners of war and displaced persons – was working hard together underground. James Miller has written a wide-ranging and fascinating account of the fast-moving years when the workers, housed in often unsavoury and utterly basic conditions, laboured twelve hours or more a day to create tunnels, colossal dams, pumping stations and reservoirs. Today, most of their living quarters have vanished and only a few houses remain for the handful of workers who maintain the dams and regulate the flow of water. Few people venture far enough into the heartland of Perthshire to view the Hydro boys' achievements.

Although the Hydro board's best-known constructions are in Perthshire they were by no means the first. The Blackwater Dam at Kinlochleven, was constructed in 1905, using minimal machinery. Many workers came from the Hebrides and spoke only Gaelic, so the foreman had to have a command of the language. Living conditions were appalling by today's standards. Drawing on his own first-hand experiences, Patrick MacGill's novel *Children of the Dead End* was first published in 1914. He wrote about how the navvies lived in shacks in a fairly lawless community, with around 3,000 workers living in shacks merely protected, after a fashion, with tarred canvas roofs, and with bunks often shared by three men. The bunks were arranged in tiers around the flimsy walls. Rudimentary cooking was done in a frying pan on a mud floor, in the midst of the squalor. The men simply wanted to earn as much as possible and had little knowledge of what they were creating, and did not care. MacGill described how this hard-bitten community worked amid the peat bogs and felt like 'outcasts . . . despised, rejected and forgotten. As indeed they are. Of the men who died in conditions without a nod to safely, nothing remains but a few cement headstones of the 20 or so men who lost their lives.'

For the next thirty years there was little interest in the building of dams for electricity generation, apart from a few small-scale schemes that drew power from the water of Lochs Ericht, Rannoch and Tummel, by the Grampian Electricity Supply Company which was later bought by the Scottish Power company in 1927. But all this was to change during World War II, through the vision of one man. Thomas Johnston, a journalist from Kirkintilloch, emerged as a terrier for the Labour party in the pursuit of socialist principles, and was an MP for West Stirlingshire before being asked by Churchill during the war to be Secretary of State for Scotland. One of Johnston's conditions for accepting was for Churchill to look favourably on the ideas which he put forward, and one of these was to harness Scotland's water for electricity, on a massive and nationwide scale. Surprising as it might appear now, Johnston was able to successfully inveigle this plan onto Churchill's desk in 1944. That he had such an influence on Churchill even in the midst of the war speaks volumes for his character, and was a foretaste of his tenacity in carrying out the building of the hydroelectric scheme.

Johnston's dream changed the landscape of Scotland, and especially Perthshire, possibly forever. But his determination, and the electricity eventually produced, transformed many lives in many remote areas. Furthermore, Johnston had to fight all the way to make sure that this massive scheme, in many parts of the country, would be managed under one company.

It was paramount to Johnston that the company should be a national one, and not privately owned. He believed passionately that natural resources should not be controlled by private interests. His vision was for a 'public corporation on a non-profit basis to harness Highland water power for electricity'. The organisation has come to be known throughout Scotland, with some affection, as 'the Hydro'. No matter that in the intervening years much has changed from this model, the name lives on in common parlance.

Of the many Hydro schemes in Scotland, those proposed for Perthshire encountered some of the most vociferous opposition. After a public meeting in Pitlochry, the local newspaper, *The Perthshire Advertiser*, noted that there was 'grave concern' about creating dams on the Tummel and the Garry. People were justifiably horrified, as there was a very real fear that livelihoods would be threatened or destroyed by the schemes. Upland farmers would lose valuable grazing fields, and tourists would cease to visit Pitlochry and the wonderful Perthshire scenery. The large landowners were nervous that their interests in the salmon fishing would be threatened, and it was also the very early days of the environmental lobby, which had seen wholesale destruction of the scenery for which Perthshire was famous. Letters were written to the same paper under pen names, such as 'Beauty Lover, Perth', pointing out that 'we want Scotland to be a place where we can get a job after the War'.

Further west, where the Sloy scheme, north of Loch Long, aimed to supply Glasgow with electricity, building was in a fairly remote spot, and not intrusive to so many vested interests. Perthshire was quite another matter. The dams were due to be built in the very heart of the county and were essential to the Hydro board's being able to return profits which would enable smaller loss-making schemes. A public enquiry in 1945 dragged on for months. One objector, acting for the National Trust for Scotland, added a couple of searing lines to the famous Jacobite song,

> Cam ye by Atholl lad wi the philibeg,
> Doon by the Tummel and banks o' the Garry?
> Saw ye the lads wi their bonnets and white cockades
> Leaving their land to follow Prince Cherlie?
> Saw ye the lads wi their cusecs and kilowatts
> Leaving the rivers defaced by Lord Airlie?

Lord Airlie, a member of the board, was regarded as a traitor to his class. His son was blackballed by the Perthshire Hunt. The board argued that the scheme was in the national interest and, finally, after six months of wrangling, the scheme got the go-ahead. It had been one of the most bruising battles the board had to fight, but two years later work began.

It was pioneering stuff for many of the engineers. Such was the challenge of the terrain and weather that in the initial stages, when surveying, engineer Bob Sim climbed up Ben Vorlich five times before he managed to arrive on the summit without mist clouding his view. He had to camp out in his sleeping bag on the summit to ensure success. Later, life became easier for the surveyors with the hiring of that new-fangled creation, a helicopter, which proceeded to deliver all the equipment to the 27 observation points required for surveying. However, the engineers and workers still had to plod up by foot.

One Donald Macleod perched seemingly precariously on the girders during the construction of the cement mixer housing at Glen Errohty.

Illustrating the dusty conditions endured by workers during the building of the Clunie tunnel on the Tummel–Garry section of the project.

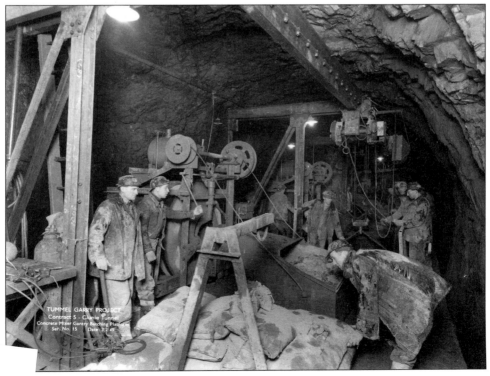

TUMMEL GARRY PROJECT
Contract 5 - Clunie Tunnel
Concrete Mixer Gantry Batching Platform
Ser. No. 15   Date: 3/2/49

On Easter Tuesday 1947, work began on the Pitlochry dam. Work progressed well, despite a flood on the Tummel in September, which managed to breach the coffer dam, causing a quarter of a million pounds' worth of damage in just one night. Teams worked to achieve records for the most rapid tunnelling and progress on the scheme. In May 1947, a team managed to advance 429 feet in one week, but soon this record was broken regularly until on 30 August 1949 the final moment came, loyally reported in the *Perthshire Advertiser* as:

> three hundred and fifty feet below Cammoch Mill near Pitlochry, a page of progress was written into history yesterday with 600 lbs (pounds) of gelignite and a piece of tartan ribbon. When the deputy agent of the Cementation Company Ltd. fired the last shot to blow the final nine foot barrier to smithereens, it had taken three years for the 300 workers to bore the tunnel from each end. The length was a little short of two miles and the two sections were less than one inch out when they met. As the dust settled, the tartan tape was hung across the gap and ceremonially cut.

After three years, with the aid of 300 workers, the tunnel was complete. As with much of the engineering, most of tunnels met within a few inches of one another, which was a testament to the accuracy of the surveying calculations. Such precision was mirrored right across the scheme.

For the workforce, leisure time was brief, and many lived life to the full. Compared to the average weekly wage for man in agricultural employment of less than £5 for a 48-hour week, the Hydro boys could earn £15 to £20 per week by doing double shifts, while the tunnel builders, who were the highest earners, would have pay packets of four or five times that amount slapped into their hands. Some turned to hard drinking, but although the discipline in the camps was severe for miscreants, most stuck it out. Those that breached too many rules would be sacked on the spot, but most remembered it as a time of great camaraderie, when differences in nationalities were forgotten, and the covering up of workmates' misdemeanours commonplace. Drink appeared to be main culprit when it came to fights and disturbances, and one famous time at Tummel Bridge, when a water distillation apparatus went missing, it transpired that it had been 'borrowed' by an enterprising man who made moonshine

Loch Tummel before the hydro dams were constructed. The water level rose above the wooded inlets in this picture, which have vanished.

in the woods by using the steeped liquid from a concoction of prunes, potato peelings and other vegetable matter in a big zinc tub. Gambling was frowned upon, but still took place regularly. Entertainments were held in various village halls, and for others the weekends were spent in the surprising pursuit of beautifying the grounds surrounding the huts. Suddenly flowers sprouted in the mud and beaten earth. Someone had the bright idea to offer a monthly prize for the best-kept hut, and the powers-that-be were taken aback by the numbers who took part in the competition.

The Hydro boys, thousands of them, came and departed. They lived in villages which no longer exist, and their legacy is only visible above ground. True to predictions, the Hydro schemes brought easier living conditions to hundreds of thousands of homes. The scarring of the landscape healed, hiding away the remnants of the camps, but one building outlived them for several years before also disappearing.

This was the unlikely construction in Pitlochry of a Roman Catholic chapel, called St Bride's Church, in 1949 by a group of Irish Roman Catholic workers both for their own use and for any local who wished to attend. The church building rose alongside the new, higher Loch Faskally, which the workers had played such a key role in creating. Naturally the company backed the initiative to build the church, ever pleased to be associated with anything unconnected with drinking or gambling. The frame was timber, set onto concrete foundations, and it took two years of part-time labour to complete the construction. Although a full-time priest was appointed two years later, many of the men had moved on, their employment in the area having come to an end. But the church stood as a reminder of their labour until it burned down in August 1965. A new church now stands on the original site.

In the meantime, another church, this time from the Church of Scotland, decided to re-locate a school from Aldour, south of Pitlochry, to a new site at Port na Craig, close to the present Pitlochry Theatre. The tin structure of Ardour School had been originally built as a school for travellers' children at Pitlochry. It too has now vanished, as has the 'experiment' to teach travellers' children separately from others in the area. As for fears that Loch Tummel would rise 17 metres, in the end the level did rise, settling at around 5.2 metres, not nearly as high as the nervous residents of the area had feared, and created an island from a promontory, now called Dun Island. Visitors flock to the Queen's View to gaze at Loch Tummel and the mountains in the distance. Despite gloomy predictions that the loch would never be the same again, the view is just as beautiful and spectacular as it ever was, but with an underlying use as an energy source.

CHAPTER 4

MONSTROUS MANSIONS, LOVE NESTS AND HAUNTED HOUSES

Around 29 mansion houses in Perthshire have vanished or linger only as rubble, or soar as ruins and are uninhabitable. Much of this sorry tale of destruction took place between 1949 and 1969. What is astonishing is that so many mansions remain, altered or reduced in size but still in use, so therefore only 'lost' in the sense that they are no longer used as the seat of a family or the centre of an estate. A conservative estimate lists the number of Perthshire mansions built or replaced on the site of existing houses in the late eighteenth and nineteenth centuries at around 100.

A plethora of elaborate and fanciful mansions of Perthshire was created at the height of the Victorian 'Balmoralia' fashion, an extravaganza of turreted exhibitionism. In some cases modest houses once owned by families who had occupied their acres of Scotland for centuries were taken over by new wealth from the cities. There is evidence that history was merely repeating itself.

For some of these wealthy newcomers, life was not without disasters in their new homes. Fire ripped through a few country houses, usually causing their destruction. For some remaining ancestral owners, the convenience of an 'accidental' fire rid the family of a ruinously expensive millstone, which is how many mansion-house owners felt after World War II. Other reasons for fire-damage were extraordinary and unpredictable.

Aberuchill, by Comrie, and the House of Ross, within the village of Comrie itself, were both set on fire by suffragettes. Aberuchill Castle dates from around 1596 when a son of Campbell of Lawers built a fortified house, now encased within the main house, which was extensively enlarged in the mid-nineteenth century. The house had been well fortified in its early days as attacks by the MacGregors were feared by the Campbell family. Robert Burns visited on his tour of the Highlands, and was unimpressed by his chilly welcome. Eventually the house passed to a Manchester cotton magnate, George L.L. Dewhurst, whose name would have been familiar to any nimble-fingered seamstress until the end of the twentieth century. The Dewhurst name was emblazoned on the end of millions of spools of thread.

The House of Ross was constructed in 1908 for Douglas Maclagan, a Glasgow stockbroker who took advantage of the efficient railway connections to build himself a country retreat within easy reach of Glasgow. Suffragettes attacked the house one night in 1914, setting it on fire so effectively that much of the house and most of the contents were lost. As the local fire brigade consisted of a handcart carrying a few lengths of hosepipes and manned by the local water inspector and street cleaner, their manpower swollen by a few passers-by, it was hardly surprising that the fire blazed out of control. Poignantly and with tragic irony, the house was the family home of Miss Nan Maclagan, a keen, although non-violent, member of the suffragette movement. It is thought the arsonists confused the House of Ross for Auchenross, home of local lawyer Balfour Mellville, who was a fierce opponent of the suffragette movement.

The fire-raisers then turned their attentions to nearby Aberuchill, where they believed Lloyd George would be staying, but with less devastating results. But this was merely a stay of execution, as almost 80 years later it was extensively damaged by another fire, this time accidental. Both houses were rebuilt, but their historic interiors have gone forever.

Within a few miles of both houses, near Comrie, another grand house has also vanished due to fire. All that remains of Dunira today are walled gardens and a gatehouse. The mansion house itself, set amid the Dunira estates which had been bought by Viscount Melville in 1784 from the Drummond family, was sold by his son, the second viscount, to a relation, Sir Robert Dundas. In the 1850s and 1860s, Sir Robert created the walled garden which still survives today. Eventually Dundas sold this house and part of the estate to George Alexander Macbeth, a Glasgow shipping magnate, who gifted it as a wedding present to his son, William.

Despite World War I, or maybe because of the buoyant income generated for shipbuilders during the war years, William altered the house, and constructed more terraced gardens between 1920 and 1922.

During World War II, the house became a convalescent home for injured military personnel, and the family moved into the home farm. By 1947, after major refurbishments, the Macbeths were anticipating a final move back into their home. But disaster then struck twice in rapid succession. Fire destroyed most of the house that same year, followed swiftly by William's death in October 1948. The widowed Mrs Macbeth lived on with her daughters in the home farm, selling out in 1950.

Fire also claimed Moncrieffe House, the ancestral home of the Moncrieffes of that Ilk. A clean, square, elegant house, it was built by one of the founders of the 'classical' architecture of Scotland, Sir William Bruce, in 1679, and occupied a commanding, south-facing position just south of Perth and adjacent to Bridge of Earn. The village of Bridge of Earn claims to be one of the oldest villages in Scotland. In 1957 a fire broke out and raged, tragically killing Sir Ian Moncrieffe, and leaving only the outside shell of Moncrieffe House.

Despite such a calamity the family decided to rebuild, and the modern house is a vague nod to its much more elegant predecessor, but does incorporate the seventeenth-century stone doorway. In the 1980s, the driveway to Moncrieffe House was bisected by the new M80 motorway, from which the house can just be seen from the north beyond the Bridge of Earn turning – or more clearly from the side road going due east round the Rhynd.

Six miles north of Perth, Stanley House stands as a stark ruin close by Stanley Mills. These mills were one of Sir Richard Arkwright's great achievements, on the very edge of the River Tay, and the fortunes of Stanley House ebbed and flowed in parallel with the mill business. In 1995, Stanley Mills were bought by Historic Scotland, helped by a grant of £1.4 million from the Heritage Lottery Fund, and in partnership with the aptly named Phoenix Trust. The mill buildings have been transformed into apartments, and a large section is now restored as a heritage centre. Their future appears secure.

Stanley House, seat of the Nairne family for 300 years, which sits in an astonishing position on a peninsula in the River Tay, was not to be as fortunate. According to the *Ordnance Gazetteer of Scotland* published in 1885, it was 'an ancient house dating from the first half the 15th century' with old yew trees and a beech avenue leading up to it. The name Stanley comes from Lord Nairne's mother, Lady Amelia Stanley, daughter of John Stanley, Earl of Derby, to whom the land

The Moncrieffe family pose on the front doorstep of Moncrieffe House, Bridge of Earn about 1880. Although the house was destroyed by fire in 1957, the front door surround was saved and incorporated in the 'new' house.

around Stanley belonged. They and their family were prominent supporters of the Stuarts, having fought as Jacobites in both the 1715 and 1745 rebellions. A stone on the riverbank just in front of Stanley House bears the date 10 June 1745, to serve as a reminder to all who saw it that the family were loyal to the Stuart cause.

With the construction of the Bell Mill in 1786, followed by further expansion, the Stanley Mills complex became a major player in the organised industrial production of cotton. From the early nineteenth century, though, the fate of Stanley House itself was closely linked to the production of cotton. Stanley House, along with the mills, was bought in 1823 by Denniston, Buchanan and Co. In 1876, the mills and house were acquired by Sir Archibald Stewart of Grandtully, but they were run by Colonel Frank Stewart Sandeman who became the owner in 1880. Of local origin, Sandeman had spent his early life in engineering and was a partner in a calico printers and bleachers near Bolton. He was a man of science and ahead of his contemporaries in many ways, installing both gas and electricity in Stanley House. This could have been the cause of the fire which then destroyed the house in 1887. Sandeman promptly moved to a house close by, Beech House, and the ruins of Stanley House lingered on for another 120 years.

While Stanley House is in a gentle setting, snuggled into a neat corner by the Tay, the gaunt ruins of Dunalastair, on the site of the ancestral home of the Struan Robertsons, occupy an imposing position overlooking the loch close by Kinloch Rannoch. Even in ruination there is a proud heroism enveloping the building, and the later history of the house explains this well. There had been a mediaeval tower house on the site that was burnt down after the rebellion of 1745 as the then chieftain, Alexander Robertson of Struan, was a Jacobite supporter.

A second house was built and the family lived there until the 1850s, when it seems that this house was accidentally burnt down. The 18th Chief was obliged to sell his Struan estate in 1854 to pay off debts. The new owner, General Sir John MacDonald, had a Scottish Baronial mansion built in 1859, taking the idea of stepped gables and steep, turreted roofs to dizzying heights. Shortly after MacDonald's death in 1866, his son sold the house to Hugh Tennent of the famous brewing family, who was anxious to hide the MacDonald coat of arms carved into the stone high over the front door. The gardener advised covering the offending coat of arms with a fast growing creeper to minimise the risk of destabilising the front elevation by having the stone hacked out. In 1891, the house was acquired by the chairman of the Caledonian Railway, J.C. Bunten, who upgraded this massive house by installing electric lighting. But from then on, it was downhill all the way. The house was requisitioned during World War II and was being used as a school for Polish refugees, when a fire destroyed the dining room. Finally abandoned in 1952, the contents were sold and the roof removed. It quickly became a derelict shell. But the creeper, which had masked the MacDonald coat of arms so effectively, has died back to reveal, with strange irony, the coat of arms as one of the few distinguishing features still evident in the twenty-first century.

Rannoch Lodge, not far from Dunalastair, was another house which lost its interior to fire in the 1980s. Home to a branch of the Menzies family, Rannoch Lodge received a number of eminent visitors: Andrew Carnegie, who stayed in this remote place for three months in 1901 when industrial unrest broke out in his Pittsburgh steel mills; Cecil Rhodes, after whom Rhodesia (Zimbabwe) was named and who journeyed here to draft the outline of an idea for Rhodes scholars to study at Oxford (former US President Clinton was one of them); Winston Churchill, who visited when a young man; and film star Elizabeth Taylor, who visited in the 1970s and early 1980s. In a different guise, the lodge served as a Wesleyan school during World War II. The exterior has survived, and the house has been rebuilt internally within much of the original exterior walls.

Building extravagant follies brought disaster of a different kind to a number of Perthshire landowners: financial ruin. In an area close to Dunkeld and Aberfeldy, there still lurk whispers of two great families who became locked in a race to build the most extravagant houses, a race which was loosely connected with attracting the attention of Queen Victoria.

Queen Victoria and Prince Albert first visited Scotland in 1842, and, within a couple of years, made no secret of the fact that they intended to buy a retreat somewhere in Scotland, and that the Highlands, to the north and west of Perth, was their chosen area. Many of the nobility, especially those with a large house to offer for sale, vied to attract the attentions of the young couple, often with a view to ridding themselves of a house they could no longer afford. Others hoped to raise their social standing by offering to host the couple in the grandeur of their mansions or castle, and set about enhancing them.

Murthly Castle was inherited by Sir James Archibald Steuart, who succeeded to the baronetcy at the age of 31. Its glorious situation on the banks of the Tay rivalled Taymouth, the Earl of Breadalbane's great castle upstream. Steuart began to plan a house whose extravagance would not have looked out of place in a theatre. In fact, the building was best described as theatrical. Sir James was an amateur architect whom history has judged as perhaps being more interested in the drawings than in the end result. There must have been many times in the following decades when his successors wished he had stuck to the drawings, rather than advancing onto the expensive construction of the great house.

Into this grandiose plan came the young Augustus Pugin, who

allegedly had been shipwrecked close to Edinburgh and taken under the wing of one of the great architects of the day, James Gillespie Graham. It is a fanciful and appealing, but ultimately an unlikely, story. Pugin designed much of Murthly's interior decoration, even describing the drawing room as having been designed in the style of Louis XIV. This great house was erected, complete with a domestic chapel and a central octagonal drawing room, culminating in the roof, finished in 1831, being crowned with wondrously gilded weather vanes.

At this point the construction ceased, coinciding with Sir James' marriage in 1832 to Jane, daughter of the earl of Moray. By this time James was 36 years old. As the eldest of the three brothers, he might have been expected to have married earlier and produced an heir, but sadly there were no children born of this short-lived marriage, and James died a mere two years later. Both of his brothers were pursuing unusual and eccentric lives. His younger brother, Thomas, had entered a monastery at Monreale, close to Palermo in Sicily. The brother to inherit the house, therefore, was William, who had not seen eye to eye with James, and had spent most of his time, and considerable amounts of his money, exploring America. William returned with bison, a Native American manservant, and drawings of the sights he had seen. The latter remain a fascinating pictorial souvenir of a vanishing way of life in the American West. The bison, transported in special wagons to both the estates at Murthly and Breadalbane, provided a source of mirth and awe for the inhabitants of nearby Birnam and Dunkeld. This was especially so when William's manservant allegedly harnessed them to a carriage constructed of a rowing boat on wheels and careered through the village.

But if it was thought that William had returned home merely to touch base and turn his back on James' 'palace', the facts tell a different story. There was no love lost between the brothers – William had sworn that he would never sleep under the same roof – but after James died, Pugin, who had been closely involved in the building owing to his connection with Gillespie Graham, produced drawings for additions to the house which included a 300-foot-long conservatory, with a glazed arcade towards the flower garden. William did not go on to build this new addition, but instead turned his attention to the existing old chapel in the grounds, rebuilding it and additionally creating a family mausoleum. He turned to Gillespie

Birnam Hill, at the foot of which Sir William Drummond Steuart built an enclosure in which to keep his bison imported from the west of America, and described by a passer-by, Queen Victoria, in 1840 as 'those strange hump-backed creatures from America'.

This addition to Murthly Castle, the creation of Sir James Archibald Steuart adjoined the old castle. This section of the house was demolished in 1949.

Graham to carry out this task, and the chapel exists today with its colourful Byzantine Revival icons.

The 'new house' of Murthly sat like a sleeping beauty for over 100 years, unfinished and unoccupied, alongside the old house.

There was a final theatrical moment in store for Murthly. On 26 January 1949, a local contractor called Charles Brand arrived to blow up the unfinished section of the house. Brand coined his own self-styled job description. He was 'the demolition expert for the aristocracy'. He prepared himself well, photographing each stage, thereby making a step-by-step guide for future demolition companies dealing with huge buildings, and indeed ensuring that his firm attracted as much excellent publicity as possible. The laird, Donald Steuart-Fothringham, was quoted as saying that the building had never been of any use except when it was used as an ammunition store during World War II or when a dance was held in the ballroom.

Remnants of the building are scattered throughout Perthshire. Some of the beautifully-cut stone was a used for the parapet of Dunkeld's old Telford Bridge, but the best stone went into the building of 35 new houses at Pitlochry.

Of a cluster of mansion houses in Strathearn, close to Crieff, very little remains. Luckily a large collection of photographs taken just before their destruction still exists to remind us of the magnificence of their interiors.

Abercairny was situated about three miles to the east of Crieff, and was still in the process of construction in 1842 when Queen Victoria, on her tour of Perthshire, stopped to see it. She was not exactly effusive: 'Got out a moment to look at Abercairny', was as much as she was prepared to devote to the house. Renowned Romantic landscape painter Horatio McCulloch was more descriptive: 'The situation is well chosen, commanding from the front a truly panoramic view of the Vale of Strathearn, bounded on the south by the Ochils, 10 miles distant – a great part of which is the property of the family; on the west by the mountains behind Drummond Castle and Crieff; and on the east and south the eye dwells on the rich and fertile vale from which the family derives its Earl's crest . . .'

Abercairny had, by the late nineteenth century, remained in the hands of the Morays for over five centuries. And like many of the great families, they had managed to drain away their long-held fortunes, first through the expense of building a huge house, and then on its continual upkeep.

Although the Abercairny Morays were Jacobites, and the laird at the time of the 1745 rebellion was raring to go and join the Jacobite side, James Moray was prevented from departing by the wiles of one of his servants. As the servant, an old and probably wise family retainer, was assisting his master to pull on his boots he 'accidentally' overturned a kettle of boiling water on his legs, disabling him. Allegedly, he followed up this act with the words: 'Tak' that; let them fecht wha like, stay ye at hame, and be the Laird o Abercairny.' History does not relate how his master then treated him, but the house was saved from the worst of retaliations after the failure of the '45.

The house was built of a light grey stone by Richard Crichton for Colonel Charles Moray who had already been improving the landscape surrounding his property at the end of the eighteenth

Abercairny, by Crieff, from a photograph taken on 27 October 1893.

century. The house was begun by Moray in 1804, left a shell when he died in 1810, and completed by his son, James, during the 1840s. It continued to be occupied after his death by Richard and Robert Dickson, Charles Moray's nephews. Abercairny had, like Murthly, been a long time in the building. It was in an imposing Gothic revival style. Much later, in 1869, a substantial and solid tower was addded onto one end. Although this was cumbersome in appearance from the outside, the surviving illustrations of the interior show a light and airy house.

One of the photographs of the drawing room, with its large floor-to-ceiling windows, gives the impression of a sunny conservatory, and other photos of the corridors with their Gothic vaulting, contrasting with the palest of pastel colours, the gleaming herringbone parquet floors, gilded furniture, delicate Chinese Chippendale chairs, elegant lamps and sense of space, show a lovely interior. Even the

The drawing room at Abercairny, papered in white and gold trellis, was filled with soft gilded furniture.

obligatory deer antlers punctuating various walls do little to mask its sheer prettiness.

Mark Girouard wrote in *Country Life* in 1961:

> The big drawing-room at Abercairny, however, was in a class of its own: its proportions, its colour and its decoration fused together to make a room that was a real delight to be in. By great good fortune it retained its original wall paper, colouring and curtains . . . the paper was white and gold; the curtains were of green damask . . . the room was a very light one and the crisscross of the vault combined with the diapered [self-patterned] wallpaper to enclose it in a kind of network of white and gold.

Sadly, the photographs which illustrate this description had been taken expressly to record this delightful space before its demolition.

Also close to Crieff was a not dissimilar house, Millearne. It sat in a picturesque site, due south of Abercairny, on the banks of the River Earn, and close by Kinkell Bridge. John Home Drummond, younger son of Sir George Blair Drummond, bought the estate in 1821. As he was related to the Morays of Abercairny it was perfectly logical that he would be intimately acquainted with the new house at Abercairny, and, indeed, employed workmen from there.

But there were charming differences. Millearne was smaller, but much less coherent and cannot have been an easy house to live comfortably in. When completed, the house contained not only two public staircases but also three private staircases for the servants to run up and down, unseen by the guests. The Gothic ceilings appear, in the pre-demolition photographs, to be heavier, but the stone cloister with the latticework lead glass windows was a trompe l'oeil, giving the illusion that the plaster vaulted ceilings were stone.

Millearne was exuberant with its mishmash of roofs, individually carved with a variety of chimney styles, and its quirky and varying ceiling heights permitting daylight to flood in from different directions, owing to the disparity in the sizes of windows. The interior was furnished, surprisingly, with late Georgian furniture rather than Gothic-style furniture which would have sat easily within the house. It was a house that appeared to have evolved piecemeal – as indeed it had – rather than according to an overall master plan. The owner, John Drummond, was very much a hands-on builder.

In one of the final photographs, taken from a tower, one can see the roofs of varying pitches, topped with slates of various shapes. There are circular chimneys with multiple carvings and decorations, most of differing heights. Shooting upwards on various towers are stepped gables, and another roof is edged with battlements. In today's climate of stringent building control, it could well have been the subject of a 'how-not-to-build' pamphlet, and the cause of much gnashing of planning department teeth. Most of the house was finished by 1838, and after John Drummond's death, his sister, Agatha, wrote: 'This beautiful house has been a great trouble and anxiety to me, from the difficulty there has been to get it properly kept. It is quite a grief for me to see what my dear John was so fond of either neglected or ill used.' This 'beautiful house' survived for another century and a quarter, when demolition reduced Millearne, like Abercairny, to a pile of rubble.

Millearne had an exuberant number of different styles, and its complex interior contained five staircases.

Many of the lost houses of Perthshire have been described in architectural detail, but with little by way of emotion. All too often the history of the house is confined to dry records of costs. Little is revealed about how the families related to their houses. Knowledge of the occupiers of houses such as Millearne was a rarity. Agatha Drummond felt deep affection and responsibility for Millearne, and said so. Seggieden, sitting on the banks of the Tay about three miles east of Perth and opposite Elcho Castle, was also recorded in detail by the occupying family, with much affection.

As often is the case, only the growth of trees such as beeches and firs distinguishes the former site of a large house. Viewed from the main dual carriageway from Perth to Dundee, the majestic trees soaring close to the River Tay give a clue that here lay this gem of a country house, the much-loved Seggieden.

Seggieden, on the banks of the Tay near Kinfauns, was home to a talented family and the garden flowers were immortalized by an artistic daughter of the house.

Prior to the erection of this most elegant of small, Adam-style houses, on a site close to one of the many ferry crossing points on the River Tay, a building had existed since at least the thirteenth century. This was a hospice run by Augustinian monks, flourishing at least until 1559. The name Seggieden, or Suggieden, is derived from the Gaelic, meaning something along the lines of 'overgrown with reeds' or 'willow den'. Certainly the soft, swishing, gentle movement of the reeds, growing as they do to the height of a small house, would lend secrecy to one's arrival. Romantically, this inlet, snaking into the bank at Seggieden, had seen many intriguing visitors pass through. Downstream just a short distance was the small pier used by MacDuff, thane of Fife, when fleeing Macbeth's soldiers. He allegedly paid off the ferrymen with a loaf of bread, this being the only offering he possessed. It was not just any bread, though, but the loaf taken from the king's table while dining at Dunsinane where he was rudely interrupted by the arrival of Macbeth's men outside. It was an apt story, even if it grew in the telling, as Sir Walter Scott embellished the tale in *The Fair Maid of Perth* in referring to the crossing as 'The Ferry of the Loaf'. Just as romantic is the true tale that the crossing was one used by the kings of Scotland as they made their way to be crowned at Scone, by way of what was known as 'the Coronation Road'.

Several centuries later, in 1745, the area received an unwelcome visit from Government forces determined to put paid to the house, which was occupied by a branch of the Hay family, who were Jacobites. Sometime in the late eighteenth century, the new and final house was erected on the site. With simple proportions, large windows and bow-fronted façade facing onto the river and terraced gardens, it was a gentle reminder that more sophisticated times had arrived. Photographs taken at the end of the nineteenth century show a large conservatory at the west wall and shrubs clambering up the walls to the second storey, evoking an image of a homely, comfortable, family house. Seggieden was indeed exactly that, the outward appearance matching the character of the occupants. In one of the happiest of unions, the heiress of the house, Charlotte Richardson Hay had married her neighbour, the 45-year-old Captain Henry Maurice Drummond of Megginch in 1859, and they took on the name of Drummond-Hay. Henry was a career soldier, rising through the ranks to colonel, but from his travels in Britain and abroad he had developed a lifelong interest in natural history, which he passed on to all his six children. He became Honorary Curator and then President of the Museum of the Perthshire Society of Natural Science. Charlotte, although busy producing their offspring, must have also been a keen gardener and from either Henry or Charlotte, or maybe both, their children inherited their immense talent.

Four of the children were daughters – Constance, Alice, Lucie and Edith – born between 1860 and 1870. Constance was born just a year before, and Alice, one year after, another talented artist, Beatrix Potter, and their artistic achievements reflect those of Beatrix to an astonishing degree. While Beatrix painted the fungi of Perthshire around Dunkeld, Constance was painting the fungi of Perthshire around the Carse of Gowrie. Constance's illustrations of fungi now reside in the Royal Botanic Garden of Edinburgh. There is no evidence, though, that the two painters ever met.

Alice took to painting flowers, and her collection finally emerged in a book called *Creating a Victorian Flower Garden* by Stefan Buczacki, published in 1988. Edith, a younger sister, produced illustrated diaries charting the family history. Inside this happy family house, with its big hallway heated by a huge stove, and lit from above by a cupola, could be found a dining-room 'panelled with wood to the ceiling, crimson brocade curtains and pelmets, a thick green carpet and a fine old Chippendale sideboard, and chairs covered in dark crimson'.

The family flourished. Father Henry collected a prodigious number of stuffed birds to add to his herbarium, while his daughters, in contrast to the suffocating youth endured by Beatrix Potter, were presented to Queen Victoria at Holyrood, and made trips abroad to France and Switzerland. At home, they were mainstays of the community and the local Episcopal church.

At Seggieden, the garden showed little sign of garish bedding plantings, as Henry took the more relaxed planting approach pioneered by Gertrude Jekyll. The dark, ominous clouds of diminishing finances and dangerous lack of maintenance were late arriving at Seggieden, unlike many other Perthshire mansions. The house was modernised with the addition of bathrooms and electricity after World War II, and then enjoyed a new life as a school, run by Lady Margaret Drummond-Hay until 1958. But a silent killer, dry rot, was steadily eroding the fabric of the house, requiring the dining room ceiling to be supported by scaffolding. Unable to afford the rising cost of repairs, a plan to burn the house in three stages was put in place in 1970. This plan went seriously awry, and the house blazed out of control for three or four days until the bulldozers could move in. Nothing but weed-covered rubble now remains.

What should have been another home of great happiness, Lynedoch, built in a very different style and of modest proportions, has also vanished. The tale is of great sorrow. Recognisable as one of the iconic images of elegance and beauty, the portrait of The Honourable Mrs Graham hangs in the National Portrait Gallery in Edinburgh. The popular story of Mrs Graham is confined to two facts. Firstly, she was achingly beautiful and painted by Gainsborough, who made such a success of her portrait that he must have been truly smitten by her. Secondly, she tragically died at the age of 35, and her husband was so distraught that he never remarried.

Until tuberculosis claimed her life, Thomas and Mary Graham were building one of the most romantic of partially thatched *cottages orné*, described by Cecil Aspinal-Orlander's *Freshly Remembered* as a 'little property . . . situated on a hillside in the middle of an enchanting wilderness, its principal buildings – a bewitching cottage –

Balgowan House was the childhood home of Thomas Graham, soldier and local MP, whose wife the Honorable Mrs Graham, née Mary Cathcart, is depicted in one of Scotland's most iconic portraits.

overlooked the River Almond. Thomas and Mary had always thought of Lynedoch as an ideal summer residence.'

For the short 13 years of their marriage, they must have longed to transfer themselves into this creation, and Mary made several sketches of the emerging house. In the meantime they lived at the family house of Balgowan, some 12 miles due west of Perth, under the eagle eye of Thomas Graham's mother, the widowed Lady Christian Graham, who kept a sharp eye on expenses. As things turned out with her son Thomas, her judgment was ominously correct.

This enchanting rustic house, at the centre of a romantic story of a great beauty and her handsome husband, was quite an unusual building to create in Scotland at that time. This poses the question of just why the Grahams opted for such a style. The clue might lie in both Mary's and Thomas' early lives. The beautiful Mrs Graham was born The Honourable Mary Cathcart, the daughter of Charles, the ninth Baron Cathcart, who had been an ambassador to Russia. Mary and her elder sister, Jane, were married in a double wedding, with

Jane becoming the wife of John, fourth duke of Atholl. Her younger sister, Louisa, was married to Lord Stormont who became British Ambassador in Paris, and frequently attended the French Royal Court, and was thus acquainted with the royal goings-on in that pre-revolutionary era, when Versailles was at its most flamboyant and extravagant. Louisa wrote detailed and lengthy letters to Mary in Scotland, and Mary stayed with her for several months in Paris in 1777. So Mary was probably influenced both by the different styles of architecture in the Russia she had viewed in her early life, and by the ill-fated fashion of Marie Antoinette for rustic cottages at Versailles.

Thomas had also received an interesting education with romantic ideals. One of his tutors had been James MacPherson, who had written extensively about the romantic Gaelic poet, Ossian. MacPherson had become something of a household name, with a bestseller on the life and works of Ossian. Who knows? Thomas as well may have had harboured romantic notions drawn from this ancient culture.

Additionally there was emerging a vogue for *cottage orné*, and this had already reached some of the most influential and popular Scottish architects of the time, such as Robert Adam, James Playfair and Robert Clark. In fact, Clark had already built a cottage high in the woods close by their home, at Dalquharran in Ayrshire, for his sister and her husband. Sketches of Lynedoch house show a U-shaped building, with varied roof heights, of which some were tiled and some were thatched, and the addition of a large, south-facing conservatory. It would be difficult to think of a more fitting house for such a young, good-looking and fashionable couple, deeply in love. Thomas Graham was the local MP, but spent precious little time in London, preferring to be in Perthshire with Mary. But the fairy story was about to come crashing down. The young couple, who had waited so long to move, were never to realise their ambition of spending the rest of their days in Lynedoch cottage. The Honourable Mary Graham died in 1792, at the age of 35, and, without doubt, part of Thomas died with her.

The famous portrait by Gainsborough, painted when Mary was but 22 and newly married, was given to her sister. Thomas could not bear to have it in the house. Grief changed his life dramatically. He became a highly successful soldier, was knighted in 1812, and became Lord Lynedoch. Shortly after he retired, unwisely refusing a pension, he founded the United Services Club in London, and bred racehorses.

The nearby Balgowan station was a convenient stop for the occupants of Balgowan house, and, small as it was, appeared to employ four of a staff.

He flung himself into creating an enchantingly beautiful estate, and went to live in the exquisite little *cottage orné*. By the time he died at the age of 95, the loose grip he had held on his purse strings resulted in a huge deficit. Subsequently, the large part of his estate was purchased by Lord Mansfield, releasing cash to be placed into the hands of the inheritors.

Perhaps his mother had been correct, and he had lavished too much unwisely. Few traces remain of the house planned and constructed so many years before. So the story might have ended and all been forgotten. The unlikely cottage, the product of many ifs and buts, with possible influences from Russian dachas, Marie Antoinette's dreams of a rustic idyll, and a highly romantic marriage, is no more. But the very beautiful and Honourable Mrs Graham takes pride of place in Scotland, ensconced as she is within the National Portrait Gallery, and her image carries with it the provision that the portrait shall never leave Scotland.

Of Balgowan House, the ancestral home of the Grahams, in which Thomas and Mary planned their cottage and from which they longed to escape from the elder Mrs Graham, even less of a reminder exists. The original Georgian mansion, plain, simple and three storeys high, was replaced by a turreted baronial building in the nineteenth century, and this in turn was blown up by the army in 1948.

Whereas Lynedoch was situated to the west of Pitcairngreen, and Balgowan to the northwest, a further house existed between Pitcairngreen and Bankfoot: Nairne House, in Strathord. However, not a trace remains. The grand house was situated just to the north of the present-day watermill, on the Ordie Burn one mile to the west of the present A9 and a mile and a half to the south of Bankfoot. It was demolished in the mid-eighteenth century.

Ballechin, a house with a more disturbing history, was situated in a position overlooking the Tay between Strathtay and Ballinluig. A corner of Ballechin House still exists, but this building appears to have been demolished with good reason. Ballechin is from the Gaelic meaning the 'town of Erchie'. In past centuries, the house passed through several tragic incidents, one of which involved murder. The master of Ballechin discovered his fiancée had another suitor. The young man displayed the heart of his rival on his sword to the young girl. Not surprisingly, she promptly disappeared, although whether voluntarily or by force was not recorded.

The house remained in Stewart hands, despite the support they gave to the Jacobite cause. In 1806 a replacement house was built on to the site of the original buildings, a classically-neat Georgian three-storey house. In the same year that the house was built or finished, a son was born called Robert, who joined the East India Company, leaving for India in 1825, and returning 25 years later, on inheriting the house and estate. He brought into the house more than just a whiff of the east. Many years of influence of different religions added to the deeply-held Roman Catholic faith he already possessed. Local rumour had it that he was a strong believer now in transmigration, the belief that after death the soul passes into the body of another person. This was odd enough, arriving in a rural stronghold of traditional religious beliefs, but stranger still was his scorning of nearly all human company in favour of dogs, of which he acquired 14. Two companions became closest to him. One was his favourite black spaniel, and the second, his housekeeper, Sarah Nicolson. His strong

Nairne House at Strathord, just to the west of the present A9 and close to Bankfoot, of which not a trace remains. Also known as the House of Nairne.

religious principles did not seem to deter him from temptations of the flesh, as this maid died mysteriously at the age of 27 in his bed, in 1873. Major Robert Stewart was her senior by 40 years. The following year he was dead also, and his remains were interred alongside Sarah in Logierait churchyard, he having left word that he intended to return to Ballechin House in the guise of a black dog.

His nephew, John, inherited the house and a clear distaste for his uncle's ideas. He promptly embarked on a shooting spree, commencing with the black spaniel, presuming this would be the very dog in which his uncle would return to Ballechin, and followed this with the slaughter of all the other dogs of his uncle's pack. He was also a devout Roman Catholic, and a cottage in the grounds was converted as a retreat for nuns. His sister Isabella had taken Holy Orders and become a nun, her name in religion being Sister Frances Helen.

Ballechin House over looking the Tay between Strathtay and Ballinluig was a house of mystery, ghosts, scandal and intrigue.

With the dogs gone and the house cleared, John Stewart must have thought that the strange influences of his uncle Robert had all been eradicated. But far from it, the influence was only just beginning. When clearing out the old man's study, John's wife became aware of an overpowering smell of dogs, and on opening the window to allow in some fresh air, she felt a dog brush against her leg, but of course no dogs still existed. Further noises such as thuds, raised voices, and guns being fired compounded the eerie sensations which lasted over several years, prompting the Stewarts' governess to leave. Father Haydon, a local priest, came to stay and spoke of thuds and dogs scraping against the door, and in a chance encounter with the said governess discovered that they had slept in two of the rooms most prone to strange noises. Odd happenings increased. Discussing estate matters with his agent in the old study, John Stewart and the agent heard loud thumps coming from inside the room, but were unable to trace them. Stewart died in an accident in London a very short time later.

Not surprisingly, the family might have felt that they had had enough of Ballechin House and its problems, and they let it to an army officer and his family. They stuck it out for eleven weeks before they too relinquished the lease, having now endured sheets being pulled off beds, rustling of silk dresses on the stairs, limping footsteps, and all the cacophony of thumps, thuds and strange noises. Major Stewart had apparently returned from India with a limp, and the limping footsteps had now become a regular occurrence.

By 1896, the Marquis of Bute swept into this strange mélange, not as a tenant in the conventional sense, but in order to study the ghostly presences, to which he had been alerted by none other than Father Haydon. The presence of apparitions was a great interest to Bute, and to assist him in the process of discovery or understanding of the phenomena he recruited two investigators, spiritualist Colonel Lemesurier and an American woman, Miss Ada Goodrich Freer. They embarked upon their investigation with determination, and eventually she produced a book, *The Alleged Hauntings of B– House*, implicating the collusion of Lord Bute in their investigations, which in itself caused a mild ripple of scandal, but it led to the book's becoming the model for a later one by Harry Price, *The Most Haunted House in England*.

The thumps and thuddings and strange noises were regarded with less suspicion by the more level-headed residents of the area. Water pipes, they concluded, would clearly account for the background effects. The pretty Georgian house, however, was doomed to be abandoned in 1932 and demolished in 1963.

A much more imposing house than Ballechin, Dupplin Castle was described by Francis Hindes Groome in 1885, in his *Ordnance Gazetteer of Scotland* as

> a noble mansion of Lower Strathearn, in Aberdalgie parish, Perthshire, 1 mile NE of Forteviot station, and 5 miles SW of Perth. Standing within a half mile of the Earn's left bank, amidst a large and finely-wooded park, it succeeded a previous edifice, destroyed by fire in 1827; and, built during 1828–32 at a cost of £30,000, is a splendid Tudor structure, commanding a view of nearly all Strathearn, and containing a library famous for rare editions of the classics.

Groome was also at pains to detail the breeding of the then owner, George Hay, eleventh earl of Kinnoull (created in 1633) and Viscount Dupplin (created in 1627), and who, born in 1827, succeeded his father in 1866. Dupplin's history was ancient. In its vicinity, on the night of 12 August 1332, the Battle of Dupplin Moor took place. Chronicles of the time described Edward Balliol, the 'disinherited barons', and their English army of around 1,500 to 2,800 archers and foot soldiers, and how they surprised and routed a much larger host of perhaps 15,000 Scots under Donald, Earl of Mar, the new Regent of Scotland. The English longbow proved a merciless weapon of war; Mar was slain, and Scottish losses were terrible.

Centuries later, on 6 September 1842, Dupplin Castle was honoured by a passing visit from Queen Victoria and Prince Albert. Afterwards, the family who had owned the castle sold it on to the Dewars, whom they would have regarded as upstarts from Aberfeldy, and indeed, worse, 'in trade'. The trade was whisky.

John Dewar, the son of a farmer from Aberfeldy, established in 1846 a wine and spirit business in Perth, naming it after himself: Dewar's. Through his production of an excellent quality of local whisky, the business, though small, had achieved moderate success within 20 years.

John senior died in 1880, leaving control of Dewar's to two of his children, John, who became a partner at the age of 24, and 17-year-old Tommy, who joined the business in 1881. An effervescent partnership had been born. John was the soundest of men, an excellent judge of character, and a financier with a steely sense of efficiency and organisation. Tommy was a born salesman and marketer. This duo transformed a successful but modest business into an international contender in the field of whisky production. They bottled their whisky, as opposed to selling it in barrels, and boldly labelled it with the Dewar name. Whisky did not have the cachet of brandy, being viewed as a drink for the common man, until the *phylloxera* insect began to devastate French vineyards in the 1870s, eventually causing stocks of brandy to run out. Waiting in the wings was Tommy Dewar, who convinced the great gentlemen's clubs of London, and further afield, that his whisky was a suitable drink for their members. He re-packaged the image of whisky as a sophisticated product. It was one of the all-time great marketing ploys. Then, in 1892, he took off on a world tour, set up agents all over the world, persuaded the then US President, the little-known Benjamin Harrison, to sip a glass or so, and the whisky became a firm favourite in the White House. While Tommy was flamboyant and lived mainly in London, John, the solid, dependable and astute businessman, sought a suitable mansion near Perth, and his choice fell upon Dupplin Castle.

Dupplin had been built in 1832 by William Burn, in a Tudoresque style, with each elevation presenting a different appearance. Lord Cockburn, the Solicitor General for Scotland, who visited in 1845, commented with approval that, 'The house both inside and out is excellent. One of the few modern houses not absurdly large. It seems to me Burn's best.' In the long run, even the modesty of the mansion and the Dewar millions were unable to save Dupplin Castle. It would suffer an interior fire in 1927 that left only the staircase intact and was finally demolished in 1967 to make way for an even more modest house to be built in its place.

If beauty is in the eye of the beholder, then the monumental Duncrub House raised the prose of Thomas Hunter, writing in his 1883 book on *Woods, Forests and Estates of Perthshire*, to giddy heights of admiration.

The style of the architecture is Tudor Gothic, actually ornamented, and the stone used is from a quarry on his lordship's estate – the

Dupplin Castle by Forteviot was built by William Burn for the then Earl of Kinnoull in 1828–32 at a cost of £30,000 and demolished in 1967. View from north-west 1911.

windows, doors, etc., being finished with the beautiful white stone of Dunmore. The exterior is lofty and imposing – in some parts three storeys high and in other places two storeys; while the kitchen entrance, offices etc., carry down to a single storey forming a very appropriate flank to the main body of the building. The Gables stepped, and the skyline generally is very effective from the different innovations of the various parts of the house. The main entrances through a magnificent porch, 30 feet in height, and richly carved throughout.

The total length of the principal front is 272 feet, and of the west front 160 feet, including the chapel which forms the most graceful termination. [Only this 'graceful termination' remains today.] On this side one of the bay windows has a handsome flight of steps. There are four fine towers, the principal one over the entrance bedding a lofty flagstaff. Both the exterior and interior of the house are finished in the most expensive and elaborate manner – no material but the very best having been used and every salient point richly ornamented with carving.

On entering the porch . . . attention is first attracted to animals in stone on either side of the doorway – the one of the right bearing the word 'Welcome', and the one on the left the word 'Farewell'.

Duncrub, near Dunning, the home of Lord and Lady Rollo, was a replacement for another house on the site, and boasted of a staircase with a bronze balustrade and a brass corona lit by 30 jets of gas. (Photo by Magnus Jackson)

Two huge lamps placed on the stone buttresses on the porch carried stone images of Lord and Lady Rollo, being 'excellent likenesses'. The author went on to explain that: 'Previous to the demolition of the old pile, Lord Rollo, in 1858, commissioned the eminent ecclesiastical architects, Messrs Haberson and Pite of London to design a little chapel near the mansion.'

Shortly after the building of this little chapel, Lord Rollo resolved to put up a new mansion house, because 'the old house was a great age, the date of its erection being lost in the mists of antiquity; and it was not only a most inconvenient structure, but it was out of harmony with the beautiful grounds by which it was surrounded'.

How times change. No matter how unfashionable and ancient the old house must have been, the style of architecture Lord Rollo chose was, to twentieth-century taste, inelegant, ponderous and depressing. The interior of the chapel, with its stained glass presenting a 'dim religious light, which pervades the interior', was the starting point for Lord Rollo's new house. 'The bronze staircase reached from the corridor through the two very richly carved Gothic arches. The stair is about 6 feet broad, with bronze balustrade, and runs round three sides of the hall, which is lighted by a very large traceried window, which can be filled with stained-glass. . . . From the centre of the ceiling, which is of richly carved wood, hangs a very handsome brass corona, lighted by some 30 jets of gas, and having, when lit, a gorgeous appearance.' The magnificent Victorian house had 50 rooms and more windows and doors than days in the year. To achieve this creation, money appeared to be no object. Further extravaganzas appeared within. 'The main drawing room was the most spacious apartment, we hear over 33 feet long and 22 feet broad, and this was as one of the suite of rooms which extended to 105 feet in length.'

John Rogerson Rollo, who spent so much money erecting this enormous monster of a house (or 'this magnificent mansion'), could trace his ancestry back to the eighth century. Eric Rollo had obtained a settlement in Normandy as early as the eighth century and an Eric de Rollo accompanied William the Conqueror to England in 1066. This Rollo lived to be 98 years old, and a portrait of him was still held by the family in the late nineteenth century. A descendant of this Eric de Rollo came to Scotland in about 1130 and from him was descended John de Rollo who settled in Perthshire on obtaining a grant of land from Robert Stewart, earl of Strathearn, later to be Robert II.

The family lived at Duncrub for many centuries, playing a major part in some of the most important events in Scotland, making prudent marriages, and rising to eminence through various military campaigns. William, the ninth baron, died in 1852, leaving an only son – John Rogerson Rollo. The following extract is taken from *Dunning: Its Parochial History* by John Wilson D.D., Minister at Dunning 1861–78.

John Rogerson Rollo, Lord Rollo, in the Peerage of Scotland, and Baron Dunning of Dunning and Pitcairns in the Peerage of the United Kingdom. Since his accession, his Lordship has greatly extended and improved the family estates, having acquired the lands of Kelty, Boghall, Steelend, Greenhill, Midgemill and Knowhead, in the parish of Dunning, and other lands in the parish of Auchterarder. He has also erected a splendid mansion at Duncrub, and built many neat and comfortable houses for the accommodation of his tenants. He takes an active interest in the prosperity of all who reside on his property, and is ever ready to promote any undertaking that he considers calculated to promote the moral or physical well-being of the parishioners of Dunning.

The original house of Duncrub, to which Robert Burn added wings in 1799, was remodelled and greatly enlarged in 1836–37 by his son, William Burn, for the eighth Lord Rollo. In 1870, Burn's house was demolished and replaced by one by Haberson and Pite. When the twelfth Lord Rollo inherited it in 1946, he decided it was too big to live in and too big to heat, though undoubtedly death duties were also a factor, and so the building and surrounding lands came to be sold in 1950. The house was demolished in that year, leaving only the chapel. Much of the stone was transported to nearby Crieff and used to build the John Smith Building at Morrison's Academy.

Stone from other houses also ended up for other uses, such as that of Lochton House. In the particulars of sale for Lochton House, dated April 1913, the situation and structure of the property was effusively described by the selling agents, Hope, Todd and Kirk WS of Charlotte Square in Edinburgh. The estate of Lochton 'is situated in the parishes of Longforgan and Abernyte in the County of Perth, about midway between Inchture and Coupar Angus – being about five miles from either place.' The mansion house 'occupies a commanding situation on the south of the estate and was erected at great expense, and is one of the most substantial and beautiful buildings of its size in Perthshire'. Quite a claim to make as the county contained around 130 mansion houses at the time.

Lochton's architectural appeal to 21st-century tastes is probably less sure, as it was built in a complex arrangement of towers, battlements and included various window styles. The architect was Charles Wilson, who practised in Glasgow, but whose commissions came from all over Scotland. His wide-ranging designs for clients incorporated Italianate flourishes, gleaned, perhaps from his early years, when, working at Hamilton Palace, he was able to study the Italian architectural drawings owned by the 10th Duke of Hamilton. Wilson's commissions ranged from Lews Castle in Stornoway for Sir James Matheson, whose fortune had been made in Hong Kong, to houses for jute magnates in Dundee.

Lochton was been built in 1852 for Andrew Brown, one of a notable Dundonian family, and was then sold in 1913 to Alfred Tosh, whose wealth came from jute. Tosh had altered the house during the 1920s, but it was in the early hours of Thursday 18 June 1931 that fire broke out and totally destroyed the interior, leaving only the main exterior walls standing.

Lochton Castle near Inchture.

Lochton House before and after the fire which ravaged the building in 1931. The owner, Alfred Tosh, then set about reconstructing the house, knocking down one section and adding a tower, but another fire destroyed the house again in the 1950s. Today it has been demolished.

The local paper, the *Evening Telegraph*, described how the local Perth and Dundee fire brigades fought the blaze, hampered by a lack of water, but almost the entire contents of the house were lost. The Tosh family were away on holiday at the time, and the house was unoccupied. Alfred Tosh then set about rebuilding the house, knocking down a section and replacing another section with a massive tower. Some of the demolished stone was used as a base for a driveway. But the house was to suffer another catastrophic fire in the 1950s, and the original splendid and flamboyant design created by Charles Wilson is now demolished.

Not far from Abernyte, Cardean House, by Meigle, of which very little remains except some stables, sits on the site of one of the great Roman camps built by Agricola in AD 84. Cardean is derived from 'Caer Dean' or 'the camp on the Dean', referring to the small river adjacent. The old bridge over the Dean is known locally as the 'Roman bridge', although there appears to be almost no proof this could be so.

A fortification also stood close by, called Baikie Castle, of which again no trace is now visible. It is probable that this stood a little to the west of the present farm of the same name. The castle reputedly was immensely strong with walls eight feet thick, and it stood in the centre of a little loch, making it a likely refuge. For at least two centuries Baikie belonged to the Fentons, an influential family from East Lothian, but no mention of the family in connection with the castle is made after 1420, and for the next 300 years, the site disappeared from historical records. There was a legend, however, that James V, the father of Mary, Queen of Scots, used to take shelter in the castle. In 1740, Baikie Castle was sold by the earl of Strathmore to David Ogilvy. Another of Strathmore's properties, Cardean House, was sold in 1785 to Patrick Murray of Simprin in Berwickshire. He appears to be the illegitimate son of Lord Elibank, a man of letters and friend of David Hume and Sir Walter Scott. While he was searching the area for a suitable mansion house to buy, Murray rented Meigle House, and while he was living there, Sir Walter Scott came to visit, and apparently wrote sections of both *Waverley* and *Quentin Durward* during his stay there. Patrick Murray bought Arthurstone, a large house which still exists close by, to which he added a wing just before his marriage. But it appears that the addition was in no great taste, and later Patrick Murray demolished the wing and transported

Belmont Castle, by Meigle, now a residential home, appears similar to this illustration of the late 1700s but now has additions to the roofline.

it stone by stone over to Cardean, at which time the house bore the curious name of Polento. At this point, however, the name Polento was changed once again to Cardean. Very little is known about the inhabitants of the house when it was known as Polento, except for a certain Captain James Ogilvy, uncle of the second earl of Airlie, who in 1662 thought that he had discovered 'an invention in secret for preserving ships from sinking'. Disappointingly, no more is known about this curious invention.

Eventually the old house of Cardean was bought by the Cox family, whose jute business in Dundee became one of the most successful in Scotland. The house then enjoyed a revival. The farm buildings were modernised, the river banks were strengthened, and the arch of the 'Roman bridge', which had been partially blown up to force people to use the new adjacent turnpike, was restored. In 1896 Edward Cox added a new wing onto the house, and two years later he bought the adjoining estate of Drumkilbo. But the end was in sight, and Cardean House was demolished in 1953, although the restored Roman Bridge remains close to the original farm buildings, and can be clearly seen from the B954.

Remnants of the picturesque Clunie Castle stand on a tiny island on Clunie Loch. While the island and castle are, in contrast to the main mansion houses of Perthshire, Lilliputian in scale, the history of Clunie Castle is substantial. The story stretches through the centuries, and even today mystery surrounds the original site of the first construction, because the tale is one of two castles. One was almost certainly built on the loch side, and the other on the island, upon which the ruins remain today.

It is not known if the island was the site of the first castle, built by Kenneth McAlpin after he managed the feat of uniting the Picts and the Scots in 843. He chose Dunkeld as his capital, but had Clunie as his hunting base. Either he built his wooden edifice on the hillock to the west of the loch, with its interesting mounding, rather like a succession of pudding basins one on top of the other, or he built it on the better defensive position of the island which has been identified as a crannog, a man-made structure which formed an artificial island on a freshwater loch.

The probabilities of a castle on the curious hill are strong. One was certainly built there and was in existence in 1141, and quite probably built some centuries earlier. Two Pictish brooches were found near the castle on the hill, both much decorated with filigree designs and both dated to around the eighth or ninth centuries. Further support for the hilltop location for the castle includes a reference to the dastardly Edward I who stayed at Clunie on his campaign through the area in 1296, when he returned to England with a souvenir, the Stone of Destiny from Scone. Rumours also abound of many deaths from the Black Death in the fourteenth century, and of bodies entombed there. Recently a dowser from the local Historical Society determined that there had been 23 burials there.

But it is the ruined Clunie Castle, still visible today on the island in the middle of the loch, which holds a fascinating history.

Of the two crannogs on Clunie Loch, one is occupied by these ruins. The castle on the island, marked on all maps as Clunie Castle and the one most commonly illustrated, was most likely to have been built partly from the masonry of the hill castle, and accounts from 1502 until 1512 record that wood came from Stobhall, and stone and lime were shipped in from across the Tay – perhaps from Fife.

For such a modest structure, its gates have seen a collection of extraordinary people pass through. The island was reputed to be a convenient hiding lair for a band of robbers in the pay of James Hering of Glasclune. These were Robin Hood-style bandits who robbed the wealthy travellers making their way from Alyth to Dunkeld delivering church funds.

Bishop George Brown of Dunkeld, who held office from 1483 to 1515 and was much interested in enhancing both Dunkeld Cathedral and caring for his clergy in his diocese, chose Clunie as a retreat for himself, and a more idyllic spot could hardly be found, even within such a wonderful part of the countryside. The Royal Commission on the Ancient and Historic Monuments of Scotland tells us that Bishop Brown was succeeded by Bishop Robert Crichton, the last pre-Reformation bishop, who handed the property over to his near relative Robert Crichton of Eliock. Crichton's son, James, better known as the Admirable Crichton (1560–82), while not born in the castle, seems to have spent his childhood there.

The Admirable Crichton was reputed to have been a youngster of formidable intellect. Educated at the University of St Andrews, from where he graduated in 1575, he then left for France, travelling

These old brick buildings were a service block for the by then demolished Dunkeld House, and lay to the north of the present Cathedral. They too were demolished around 1900.

A chalk sketch of the Gothic styled Dunkeld House in construction between 1828 and 1830, which replaced an earlier house. This one was never finished and demolished. The present Dunkeld House – now a Hotel was built in 1900.

on to Italy, visiting both Venice and Padua, and becoming a legend in his own short lifetime, writing poetry, and enjoying a reputation for astonishing physical prowess. But, in 1582, while working for the duke of Mantua, he met his death in a brawl. He was 22 years old. His life could have been easily forgotten, but the tales surrounding his exploits have lived on. In 1602 he had been posthumously dubbed the Admirable Crichton by Ben Jonson in his *Heroes Scoti,* and Sir Thomas Urquhart published a book referring to him in the title as *Discovery of a most exquisite jewel* in 1652.

Clunie Castle was in fairly good repair until the mid-twentieth century, even being freshly painted in preparation for a visit by Queen Mary in 1936. She balked, however, when invited to step into a small rowing boat to be taken across to the island, much to the disappointment of the many people who were waiting to greet her.

The loss of the castle occurred when some fishermen, who had rowed over to stay on the island, lit a fire in the Great Hall, accidentally allowing it to get out of control. The fire spread into the roof timbers and rapidly put an end to the prettiest of all the small castles in Perthshire

To the north side of Clunie Church, you stumble across the remains of boxwood hedging and various carefully constructed cut stone remains of buildings. This was probably the pleasure garden for the castle, created during the mid-1700s. Sadly, most of this has now vanished.

A building falsely associated with ecclesiastical history is Rossie Priory, on the very edge of Perthshire and but six miles from Dundee city centre. This was never a priory in the true sense of a religious building. Fancifully, it earned this description owing instead to the extravagant Gothic appearance of its south elevation. It was built for Charles, the eighth Lord Kinnaird, by William Atkinson, between 1807 and 1815, with a park laid out previously, around 1786. Only a fraction of the building remains, the rest having been demolished in 1949.

Demolition experts put paid to a spate of properties in the late 1940s and early 1950s, culminating in what appears to be a frenzied demolition of at least a dozen houses in the 1960s and early 1970s. Many of these houses were in a run-down state, with dry rot invading the fabric of their structure. Others were impossible for their owners to maintain, owing to the immense costs of repairs such as re-roofing. At the end of World War II, few staff could be found to help run these large houses. A way of life, in which huge house parties would assemble for weekends, or during the shooting season, had come to an end. Furthermore, it was largely accepted that demolition was the inevitable finale. Very few spoke out in opposition, and even if they voiced concerns, they were easily silenced by being asked just what they could do to justify saving them. Many houses had been requisitioned during the wars, and had suffered much damage but, all in all, these 'white elephants' were recognised as being no longer of use in the twentieth century.

On a far lesser scale to the great houses of Perthshire were modest buildings constructed of corrugated iron, commonly known as 'tin buildings'. For at least 100 years these buildings were an inexpensive godsend for many. Some would say they littered the countryside.

Others prefer to look back with nostalgia on a landscape speckled with the distinctive tin roofs, some painted with protective red iron paint the colour of tomato paste, and others clad in the darker, gingery hue of simple rust. Their advantage was the ease with which they could be erected, and the price and the speed of their building added to their undoubted attraction.

Henry Robinson Palmer (1795–1844), the founder of the Institute of Civil Engineers, is credited with inventing the process of corrugating iron which renders the sheets much stronger. Prefabricated buildings of corrugated iron were shipped to outposts of the Empire by manufacturers such as Boulton and Paul, who later produced warplanes and kitchen units, as well as a range of prefab, iron-clad houses up to the beginning of the twentieth century.

Corrugated iron was to become the replacement roofing of choice on the remaining stone-walled long-houses and black houses of the Highlands and Islands and bring an end to the backbreaking and frequent job of re-thatching with heather or turf. Historic Scotland deliberately kept the tin roof on the long-house in its ownership at Killin, Perthshire.

Suki Urquhart has written lovingly about her battle to save the tin church, next-door to her house in Aberfeldy. It was one of the many which were commonly called 'tin Tabernacles', and she wrote that

Is it a tin shack or a cherished architectural gem? Opinion will always be divided over the merits of corrugated iron buildings. The versatility of tin and the different uses it can be put to, since its invention in 1829, has created a flourishing architectural heritage. All over Scotland it is possible to find examples of custom built tin huts for shooters, fishers, bowlers and curlers, game larders and boat-houses, schools, churches, cottages and village shops, station huts and halts as well as other treats such as the odd, rare mobile shepherd's hut. Some boast decorative barge boarding, ornate roof ridging and well-crafted doors and windows, most are characterful and their colours fade beautifully.

But most have vanished.

Perthshire has lost many corrugated-iron buildings. In losing these buildings there is also the loss of their history. Almost all the old buildings, such as the one in Glen Quaich shown overleaf alongside the farm buildings at Tirchardie, are lying little-used and unloved.

Situated in Glen Quaich, this corrugated iron farm building reflects the more elaborate use of this popular material, while the interior is an intricate system of wooden struts.

The images here of a beautifully built wood and tin farm shed illustrate perfectly the care and pride that some farmers bestowed on their buildings. The exterior was crafted to make it a very attractive addition to the farm. Today perhaps farm buildings rise up to be strictly utilitarian buildings but, ironically, most of them are constructed of a modern version of the old 'wriggly corrugated iron' much used for generations.

As Suki Urquhart points out:

To a whole generation scarred by two World Wars, corrugated iron is associated with wartime austerity – 'elephant' and air-raid shelters, Nissen huts and barracks and postwar building using cheap materials. To a younger generation it conjures up shantytowns and slums in third world countries, with their patchwork of recycled tin sheets. To yet another group, tin is purely for utilitarian agricultural sheds and warehouses. But for some who have travelled the world, brightly coloured tin buildings are a legacy of the Scots involvement in colonialism abroad and conflict in the church; factors that combined to create a market for kit buildings around the Empire as well as in Scotland. These timber-framed, ironclad buildings were shipped to all parts of Britain and its Empire, including Australia, New Zealand, the West Indies, Africa, India and North America. Sending flat pack buildings abroad has been going on since the 18th century.

The tin church which Suki Urquhart fought to save is Our Lady of Mercy Roman Catholic Chapel near Aberfeldy. It was built in 1884 and funded by the Earl of Bute, whose money enabled many tin churches all over the country to be built. As she remarks, 'Possibly because people are more reluctant to pull down churches, more of these seem to have survived intact and there are many examples in various stages of dilapidation to be found all over the U.K. The famous tin church on Orkney, built and decorated by Italian prisoners of war, has become a national treasure. Probably the largest tin church still in use is the one at the notorious Deep Cut Barracks in Surrey, while more elaborate, but of a similar size, was the long gone tin cathedral in Oban built in 1878.'

The tin church built in Pitlochry for the Hydro workers in the 1950s perfectly illustrated how these inexpensive buildings sprang up.

The River Tay below Kinfauns, close to the landing place when crossing the river by the Coronation Road.

CHAPTER 5

ROYAL ROUTES, ABUNDANT
FERRIES AND TRAINS WITH SAILS

Royal associations with Perth and Perthshire stretch back for at least a millennium. From as early as 843, the kings of Scotland were crowned at Scone and a special road led there, known as the 'Coronation Road', along which those who were about to be crowned would travel.

However, the Coronation Road is little known in Perthshire today, and no longer is a well-used thoroughfare. Only some sections of footpaths carry signs to indicate its presence, but even if you locate these and follow the route around Perth and Scone, this is but a fraction of its original length. The entire road led all the way from the palace at Falkland to the palace at Scone, and its history tells of ghosts, murders, biscuits, and triumph.

Charles II, in 1651, was the last king to make the journey along the Coronation Road, but his crowning was to be only a brief interlude before his exile to France.

After the execution of Charles I in 1649, Cromwell had marched north, defeated the Scots at the Battle of Dunbar on 3 September 1650, captured part of southern Scotland and seized and removed the nation's public records, although he did not manage to take the Scottish Regalia – the Honours of Scotland.

On 1 January 1651, the Scots crowned Charles II at Scone, and in July, the English army marched into Fife and then captured Perth, while the Scottish forces headed south into England, where they were defeated at the Battle of Worcester on 3 September 1651. Charles II escaped, and fled to France. The English, meanwhile, moved on to take Stirling and Dundee.

Charles II spent the next nine years in exile until, in 1660, he was invited back to London and restored to his father's throne. He always recalled with distaste his time in Scotland, apparently because the Presbyterians had lectured him constantly about morality and told him that kings were merely the vassals of God, like everyone else. As this hectoring had occurred in a chilly Scottish January, the experience had not endeared him to Scotland, and so he had no desire to go north again. Instead, Charles left his Secretary of State, John, duke of Lauderdale, to enforce his policies of royal absolutism in both Church and State.

Charles' crowning had ended the tradition, going back many centuries, of using the Coronation Road. With some certainty, historians agree that the route had been used between AD 700 and 1050, as the Kingdom of Scone was the likely hub around which the mysterious Picts built up their realm, the area occupying, as it did, the central position between the northern and southern Picts.

The Coronation Road was the obvious route used by the MacDuffs, thanes (later earls) of Fife, to journey from their home in Falkland Palace to fulfil their centuries-long hereditary duty to crown the Scottish kings seated on the Stone of Destiny at Scone. Although Scottish kings were crowned at Scone from 843 to 1406, their enthronement on the Stone of Destiny was only possible until 1293, when Edward I of England captured the stone in 1296 and took it to Westminster.

The road into Abernethy is marked by an ancient round tower, past the hill fort on Castle Law. The tower was built in the eleventh century and was thought to have been where a look-out was kept for grave-robbers. It is likely, however, that some structure of religious significance has been in place there for a lot longer and that this would have marked the ancient track which became the Coronation Road.

In fact, evidence of this is found in the following tale taken from the ancient Ogham script tablet found in Newport, Fife, in 1958, although sadly now lost:

King Alpin's Dalriadan horde laid waste the fields of the Picts in the land known as Perth and Fife. The king ruled with a hand of iron, killing any prisoners and taking anything of any value from houses and hovels alike. He followed from the south the marks till he came to the river-crossing of Abernethy where he was received with great rejoicing, but in need of rest he sought shelter in a baker woman's house. The following day, she left home instructing her lodger, of whom she had no inkling of his identity, to keep an eye on her baking, instructing him to take care to look after the buns in the oven. But in her haste she had forgotten to add leaven to the mixture. Furthermore the king, though he agreed to do what she asked, was distracted by the impending build up of troops and the imminent battle he assumed would be within hours. He forgot to take the buns out of the oven, and was scolded by the returning baker woman.

At that instant the King's lieutenant, the loyal Lord Kintyre, came into the house. 'Sire, the enemy is in sight. We must take battle to him this instant.'

It was only then the baker woman recognised the king for who he was, and horrified, she fell on her knees. But King Alpin reassured her that it was he who had misused her hospitality. The buns, now flat, cooled and brittle, were tasted by Lord Kintyre, the King's lieutenant, who found it was crisp and broke loudly in the mouth. He ate it all and then another and then another.

'Madam,' said Lord Kintyre, 'I greatly like these biscuits of Abernethy but I must take the king now to fight the Norse raiders.'

He and the king left, carrying with them the rest of the biscuits for their men. That very day King Alpin was killed in battle with the Norsemen. The flat Abernethy biscuit, though, lives on in a few bakeries in Perthshire.

Take the A913 to the northeast out of Abernethy and turn off to the left after half a mile or so, down a minor road to Ferryfield of Carpow. The road ends at the River Earn, slightly upstream from where it joins the Tay. Ferryfield of Carpow was the main ferry crossing-point on the Earn. The river is slow-moving here, and sheep and cattle could be herded across. Eight log boats, all dated as being made between 1000 BC and 500 BC have been found, mainly in the nineteenth cemtury, in mud alongside the Tay. The latest one, found in 2001 and lifted out in 2006, was 9.25 metres (30 feet) long and made from a single piece of oak. The land around the estuary at the time of this log boat would have been occupied by settlements consisting of several houses (known as roundhouses), with small fields and pockets of woodland. The inhabitants of these small settlements would have spent most of their time farming, although they would have also taken advantage of the rich estuary environment.

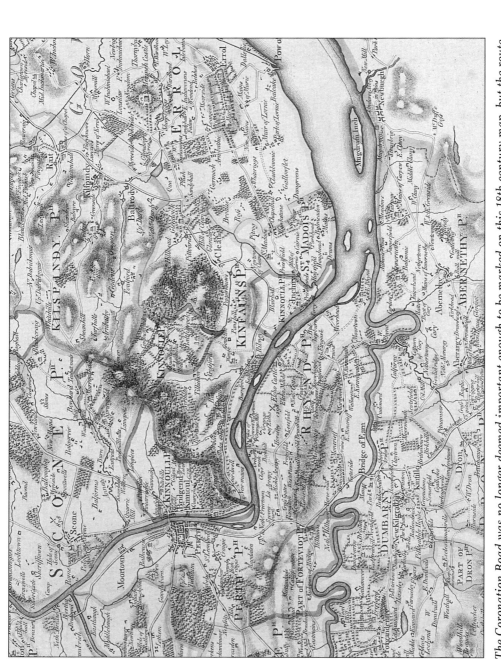

The Coronation Road was no longer deemed important enough to be marked on this 18th century map, but the route crossed over the Rivers Tay and Earn, wending its way over to Scone.

The impressive size and design of the log boat suggests that it may have been used for a variety of tasks. It could hold up to 10 or 12 individuals at a time, and is likely to have ferried people and trade goods around the estuary. It may also have been used for hunting and fishing, or, given its size, as a symbol of status. So there was every chance that this crossing of the Tay would have been used much earlier than when the route became known as the Coronation Road.

There is also the likelihood that it was used by the Romans. After crossing the Earn at Ferryfield of Carpow, the Coronation Road would then have continued on the track through Easter Rhynd and thence to Elcho Castle.

The north leg of the Coronation Road continues across the river from Elcho Castle. Today, it is only at this point that the road is sign-posted as such, as a bridleway. After landing at Seggieden, the coronation party would climb the slope from the Tay to Kinfauns Church, where they would stop for a religious service. The old church is now but a ruin on the east side of the modern church building.

The road ran through a village called Crossford, now vanished, up past the present-day Deuchny Woods and down to Parkfield Farm originally known as Lime Potts (possibly because, owing to its lack close to Perth, lime had to be brought in from Fife along this road).

The road swung through the present Pickstonhill Farm and then into Scone itself, along its present-day streets: Cross Street, Abbey Road, Sandy Road, and then west into Stormont Road and terminating at the site of the Old Abbey, hard by Scone Palace.

Much of this road through Perthshire can be followed today on foot. From Scone to Seggieden is around eight miles, and routes for the public to walk safely are on the Perth and Kinross website.

The Coronation Road isn't Perthshire's only ancient and historic thoroughfare. The 'Wallace Road' may be less well known, but its associations are equally colourful and this too can be walked as part of a 'Heritage Paths' network.

William Wallace was a towering figure in Scots history and the descriptive key to his entry in Collins Encyclopedia of Scotland runs to one word: 'patriot'. Whether he ever travelled on the road now named after him can, of course, never be totally proven, and the route itself, twining its way over the land above Glenfarg, the Wicks of

Baiglie, the Path of Dron, and eventually dropping down to the river crossing-place at Bridge of Earn, is little known today. But the road dates back many centuries, even before Wallace's birth in 1270.

The road is said to have been used in Roman times going back to the days of Agricola. Several forts were built on the hills overlooking Strathearn as a line of defence against the Caledonians who dwelt to the north.

It is also thought that Mary of Guise, her daughter Mary Queen of Scots and Lord Darnley all travelled this road as it was the most direct to Perth from Dunfermline

King Charles I in 1632 came to Scotland to receive his crown. After his triumphal entry into Edinburgh he visited Dunfermline and then made his way to Perth riding on horseback with his retinue along this road. Shortly after, Oliver Cromwell led his Ironsides along this road to his intended attack on Perth in 1651.

Later the road is associated with the struggles of the 'Forty-Five' when the exiled Stuarts made a push for the throne of Britain. The Jacobites may well have travelled up and down the road.

Despite not being made up to take coaches, the Wallace Road was shorter than the maintained Wicks of Baiglie public road (which became the turnpike in 1753) and continued to be used by gentlemen on horse, harvest workers, smugglers and numerous other travellers.

In 1787 while on his way from Perth to Edinburgh, Robert Burns detoured from the more direct route to visit Invermay, near Path of Condie, and although his visit did not merit much in the way of detail, his description of his hostess Mrs Belches was not flattering, but illuminating of his sharp eye for the attraction of the fairer sex.

'Today dined at Invermay. Mrs. Belches not very well favoured.' So she can't have been a great beauty. It was rumoured that he inscribed his name with a ring on the window of the school at Path of Condie after his visit to Invermay House.

Sir Walter Scott used the Wallace Road in 1796 to reach Invermay, a few miles west of here. He later recalled the view overlooking the hills and straths around Perth to the highlands beyond in the opening pages of his novel 'The Fair Maid of Perth', where he says that the summit of this old road is "one of the most beautiful points of view in Britain". The view, he wrote, is from a spot called the Wicks of Baiglie, now often confused with the Wicks of Baiglie road, but the road of that name is two miles to the east. His 'viewpoint', with a gap between the hills allowing the view of Perth and beyond, is likely to be between Dron Hill and Mundie Hill.

Clearly the road has a long and prestigious history. It was lined with ash and elm trees until Dutch elm disease killed off most of the elms in the 20th century and now there are only some ash trees lining the road. The section of road just south of West Dron Hill Farm is now lined by the trunks of dead trees and decaying upright trees.

Such landmarks do not denote the later roads which were built by General George Wade.

Many of these old routes were previously used as drove roads, mainly for the small stocky black cattle which survived and thrived so well on the high ground of the Highlands, and were driven down to the great trysting fields of Crieff and further south to Falkirk.

The drove roads of Scotland are evocatively and happily entrenched in the Scottish mystical history, certainly up until the end of the 18th century. But the roads themselves were not created until after the Jacobite rebellions of 1715 and 1745. The drovers knew the best ways through the hill passes and would also break away from any strictly bounded road, fanning out on either side in order to find the best grazing for their cattle as they came south. And there were many, many cattle, driven over many loosely defined paths.

In 1723 it was estimated that 30,000 cattle changed hands in Crieff. The gathering there attracted buyers from the lowlands and further south. The dealers would buy cattle in order to take them down to the rich meadowlands and pastures not only on the Scottish Borders but further south as far as Yorkshire and East Anglia where cattle would continue to be fattened up for a burgeoning market.

Drove roads, as opposed to the vague tracks, were a side product of the roadbuilding efforts of Field Marshal George Wade, Thomas Telford and John and Joseph Mitchell, whose remit had been to build stable and organized roads to improve communication in the Highlands, thus allowing easier military control. The fact that these roads would offer themselves as drove roads was an additional bonus. It was, typically, a misunderstanding by the incomers of the shrewd Highlanders.

At first the landowners adjacent to these new roads rubbed their hands in glee at the prospect of being able to restrict these cattle dealers, and their grazing, while very conveniently building shelters and inns so that they could extract hostelry charges.

The 'old' Spittal of Glenshee hotel in the latter half of the 19th century. Originally a 'hospice' or place of refuge, overnight stay or lodging house, the hotel, much changed, remains popular today.

Kirkmichael was a busy place with cattle and their drovers passing through, and enjoyed a week-long market, although this had vanished by the time of this photograph in the 1890s.

The Meikleour Inn, just south of Blairgowrie, is almost unchanged; only the stopping off point for a stagecoach and horses has changed to that of a halt for the sparse bus service.

One of the famous drove roads through Perthshire came down from Deeside, over Glenshee and the Cairnwell, stopping off at Kirkmichael, which enjoyed a week-long market. Local farmers would bring their cattle to the drovers, and often sell them immediately, so that the drovers then had the risk of taking them further south to markets in Crieff or Falkirk.

W. Marshall, in *Historic Scenes in Perthshire* (Edinburgh, 1881) wrote: 'When the drovers . . . make their appearance in the Highlands which always happens during the latter end of April or beginning of May, they give the intimation at the churches that upon a certain day and in a central place they are ready to purchase cattle from any who offer sale.'

From Kirkmichael, the drovers proceeded over the hills through Glen Derby, over by Loch Broom down to Netherton of Dalcapon. Here are still to be seen the remains of one of the 'raiks' or resting places.

By the mid-1830s, the droving was at its peak, and the cattle were joined by sheep on their way south. Generally the herds would number up to 300 animals, with each drover plus his dog in charge of 50 or so animals. Gathering more cattle as they went south, the commotion and noise must have been ear-splitting to the locals, unused to such a massive influx of strangers passing by.

The track wended its way south, and on the hill just beyond Loch Ordie, known as the Cross o Coupar, a market had traditionally taken place, and the area was known as the 'Drover's Park', so Tulliemet farmers could bring their cattle for sale.

Convenient as some of the bridges and stone causeways were to the drovers, this also meant that their cattle, only used to soft ground, has now to be shod. So yet another opportunity arose as blacksmiths positioned themselves just before the hard stone roads began in order to shoe the cattle.

The great gatherings at Crieff which became three-day parties, producing not only great storytellers, much music and merriment and the copious consumption of ale and whisky, were coming to an end. Up until the end of the 18th century, the great cattle trysts took place just below the Highland line because the Lowlanders feared venturing too far north into the unknown homelands of the fearsome Highlanders. Both sides found it convenient to meet at Crieff, and this high spot of the year produced a bonanza for the small town.

The wars within Europe from 1750 right up to the defeat of Napoleon in 1815 produced a hungry army. The Scottish cattle were ideal in meeting that demand. But then, with Napoleon secured on St Helena, peace broke out in Europe and the very high demand fell. As the country became even more accessible, an organized, structured type of cattle mart was created in Perth in the middle of the 19th century, and the era of the drove roads disappeared.

The cost of travel in Perthshire, as elsewhere, was expensive. Tolls existed on most roads, if travelled by coach. And tollhouses have mainly vanished, lost in road widenings and improvements. In 1799 the travel costs of Captain Allan Macpherson of Blairgowrie were carefully recorded by himself. Accompanied by his wife, Eliza, one servant, his daughter, Harriet, and possibly his son, William, both of them teenagers, the cost of travelling to London totalled £56 and took all of 15 days. The return trip cost £43 9s 5 ½d. This was around the wage earned by a miner over the year. At a total of around £100, this would have been two years' wages for a teacher, or about three quarters of the annual earning power of a doctor. At this time an ordinary soldier in the Perthshire Fencibles was paid 1s a day. An agricultural worker was paid about 23d, or just under 2s a day.

The Macpherson family departed on 16 September 1799, and took 15 days to reach London, arriving on 6 October. On the first day they travelled a total of 14.5 miles, paid 1s 6d for porterage over the bridge on the Isla (probably by Ballathie) and stayed in or close to Perth, at MacDougal's Inn for the night. With breakfast the next day, the bill, to include the chambermaid (2s 6d) and ostler (1s) paid totalled £2 14s 4d.

The next day they reached Auchterarder, where eating (12s), port (3s 6d), servants' meals (4s 6d), waiter (1s), chambermaid (3s), ostler (6d) cost a total of £1 11s 6d. They had covered 14 miles from the previous night. By 19 September, they had reached Dunblane, lodging at the north end of the bridge at the inn of Mrs Thomas, at which point to the cost of the lodgings was added corn (3s 6d) and hay (2s), chamber maid (2s) and ostler (6d). The next days were spent as guests of Sir John and Lady Murray at Cambus-Wallace, and then, on 21 September, they left for Stirling, by which time they had spent £6 1s 9d.

It is humbling and extraordinary for us to realise today, having access to maps meticulously drawn, and electronic methods of not only pin-pointing our position, but guiding us towards the best possible route, that in previous centuries many folk set off with only the vaguest idea of which way to go. They relied on fellow travellers offering the correct information, and would often wander for many miles out of their way. Even in 1912, when maps were more readily available, Sir James Ramsay, a local laird and a man of considerable social standing, set off from his home near Alyth to walk to Braemar, relying only on being given guidance from the occupants of a cottage on the way. (His walk is described later in this book.) Maps were hugely expensive and only available for the wealthy, sign-posts were rudimentary and milestones were to be seen on but few of the major thoroughfares.

Although the first recorded milestones were put in place by the

All that remains of Auchterarder Castle, of which little history also exists. Most references to it only tell a skeletal tale. In 1227 Alexander II granted the canons of Inchaffray rights over Auchterarder, and the castle provided a useful resting point for Edward I of England as he strode north in 1226. The Treaty of Perth signed here by Mary of Guise enabled John Knox to gain the first State recognition of Protestantism in Scotland. When the MacPherson family passed through in 1799, the town was enjoying some prosperity with linen weaving, a dye works and a paper mill. The remaining section of the castle sits amid a farmyard just to the northwest of the main street.

Romans, who defined the centre of Imperial Rome with the 'Golden Milestone', it took until the end of the eighteenth century for milestones to be compulsory on all turnpikes, to inform travellers of direction and distances, to help coaches keep to schedule and to determine charges for changes of horses at the coaching inns. The distances were also used to calculate postal charges before a uniform postal rate was introduced in 1840.

In 1824, the cost of proceeding from Acharn, a hamlet on the south side of Loch Tay, to St Andrews was meticulously recorded by Duncan Dewar, who made the trip to study at the university. Duncan was born in Acharn, within the parish of Kenmore, on 6 March 1801. He was one of seven children, and attended school locally at Kenmore. His father was a handloom weaver and possibly a tailor as well. Almost certainly, the Dewars worked a croft and Duncan would have stayed at home until he was 18, assisting on the croft. His seven years at the University of St Andrews cost a total of £101, around £80 of which was contributed by his family, a monumental financial achievement, when the average wage of a skilled textile worker was £48 a year.

Duncan set off on foot from Acharn for the university session of 1824–25, spending a total of 2s – the same as the hay for Captain Macpherson's horse in Dunblane 25 years earlier, and much less than Macpherson's 3s 6d bottle of port. He would have set off very early in the morning, walking over the hill above Glen Quaich, down the glen to Amulree, across an unspecified hill to Logiealmond, and on to Perth. There are now several clues as to which route included the 'unspecified hill'.

Little travelled now, virtually unmarked and indistinguishable to the driver on the A822 through the Sma' Glen, the route followed by Dewar may well have been a section of an ancient road mentioned in the Chronicle of Fortingall and shown on Scobie's map of 1783 (shown in this book). This road forks off the A822 just south of Amulree, across to the isolated homestead of Girron and then turns in a south-easterly direction, joining what is now the B8063, just south of Logiealmond Lodge, and then proceeds on to probably Methven and Perth. The Chronicle of Fortingall was compiled by a succession of MacGregors between 1400 and 1597 and as the route is mentioned in this it must have been a very important thoroughfare.

Sir Peter Redford Scott Lang, the Regius Professor in Mathematics at St Andrews, who studied Dewar's account, remarked that it was common for students to meet up with one another, going from and returning to university, as the journey was long. Students from Blair Atholl walked between 60 and 70 miles in one day.

One route for students to follow was the road south of Perth called the Great North Road, today's A9, round the south side of Moncreiff Hill, onto the ferry at the southeast tip of the Rhynd, then landing at Jamesfield, and onwards through Newburgh, Cupar and thence to St Andrews.

Dewar, as other students, could complete this long trek more easily, even if it appears to have required immense physical endurance, as he would have carried almost no luggage. He probably carried merely some food for the journey. He made almost no reference, in the seven years of travelling, to spending more than a few pennies on accommodation or food en route, unlike the Macphersons. The annual salary of a teacher then was around £43 and a government clerk at the high end of the scale earned £133. Labourers and crofters could expect a fraction of this amount. So for the aspiring son of the croft, travelling was confined as far as possible to walking. Paying for overnight stays in inns was usually avoided unless absolutely necessary.

A trunk carrying all things necessary for his half year at St Andrews would be sent in advance by carriage to Perth. Inside the trunk would have been books, clothes for six months, and 'victuals'. When Dewar arrived at Perth, he would pay porterage (5d), make sure it was stowed on the steamer bound for Dundee, arrange for it to be transported onto the ferry to Newport (6d) and then arrange for a carrier to take it to St Andrews. He walked. All this was accomplished in one day.

Today, on roads which take more direct routes, the 72-mile journey from Kenmore to St Andrews could be easily driven in just over two hours. As the records of just how students journeyed must have been rare in the early nineteenth century, Professor Lang filled an entire book both analysing and commenting on Dewar's costs at university, and the details of his journeys. He assumed that Dewar must have aimed to leave home in Acharn at around four o'clock in the morning to be certain of reaching the steamer in time. Of course, the steamers were dependent on the tides, so would depart at varying times, all of which were printed in the *Dundee, Perth and Cupar Advertiser*, published each Thursday. In 1822, an advertisement in that paper enthused that 'the *Athol* of thirty horsepower and fitted in every part in the most elegant and commodious manner, with a comfortable steward's room where refreshments of every sort can be served and a select library of new publications is provided, will perform the journey from Dundee to Perth in ordinary cases in about two and a half hours, whereas her predecessor, the *Caledonia*, took four hours'.

Making his way from his home at Acharn on Loch Tay to St Andrews University in the 1820s, student Duncan Dewar would have walked along tracks just like this. This 1880s photograph is simply entitled 'A Scene in Perthshire'.

Dewar's costs for the steamboat from Perth to Dundee were 2s 6d and for the Dundee ferry over to Tayport, 6d, with the St Andrews carrier, 2s. His total journey one way cost 5s 11d, which equates to around £24 today, or £48 return. This was a hefty amount, when 52 or so miles of the 72 were done on foot.

A footnote to Duncan Dewar's canniness, contained in his accounts for the seven years of study, was his purchasing of new clothes. In the 1821–22 session he bought material for three new pairs of trousers. Two pairs were made from five and a quarter yards of moleskin, and another ready-made pair were of 'jean trousers. This stuff was a hard material like coarse gabardine cloth and about half the weight of moleskin.'

Later, he took to buying black trousers, black vests, the lining for both, as well as a pair of spats as he was preparing for ordination into the ministry. He went on to take a charge at Dull, on the north side of the River Tay, and not far distant from Kenmore, where he remained for 22 years until his retirement.

Duncan Dewar must have been exceedingly grateful that a trip on the steamer relieved him of walking the long trek through the Rhynd and into Fife, grateful that the great rivers of Perthshire provided transport and many other advantages. Their massive power and their constant movement filled the various mill lades and generated electricity for the many industries on their riverbanks. They offered fresh water for drinking, if no springs were easily accessed, were

Hostelries or houses which offered refreshment were situated along the well-trod routes. This one, offering lemonade and ginger beer to the thirsty traveller, was not an option for students in penury, such as Duncan Dewar.

much used for washing clothes and watering cattle, and came into their own as clear and convenient boundaries. Occasionally they became the first line of defence, as a flooded river was a daunting and dangerous obstacle for an enemy to cross.

But with the conveniences of the great rivers, and especially the Tay, came one major drawback for travellers. For a country dissected by so many major rivers, Scotland had fewer than 200 bridges before the seventeenth century. So, although rivers supplied many of the most essential factors to sustain life, they presented a major problem when one wished to cross over to the other bank. Folk mainly relied on their own efforts, on foot or on horseback at tried and tested crossing points. The Romans had erected a wooden bridge over the Forth at Stirling, and centuries later another wooden bridge at the same crossing was the site of the great battle in 1297 between William Wallace's Scots and the army of Edward I. The problem with wooden bridges was their flimsy construction – they could all too easily be either swept away or burnt by an enemy during times of war or instability, in which case it would be many years before the bridge was replaced. Only a couple of stone bridges were built over the Earn and the Tay, with the stone coming from quarries belonging to Scone Abbey. These earliest stone bridges were constructed in 1326 at the instigation of Robert the Bruce. The bridge at Perth was regarded by James VI as 'a most precious jewel in our kingdom and a work profitable and primely necessary to our whole Kingdom and dominion . . . for the suppression of rebels . . . and also keeping the one half of the kingdom with the other half in faith, obedience, duty and office towards us, their king'.

But the fine words and aspirations did not alter the practicalities of maintaining the two bridges. They were supposedly built on foundations constructed from clay and earth, and appeared to be in a constant state of serious disrepair, and regarded by the local populace as unreliable. They were correct. The bridge over the Tay at Perth lasted only until 1621, and for the next 150 years after its demolition, transportation returned to the old ferry system. Bridges were such an expensive proposition, a technical feat to build and a challenge to maintain, that ferry transport became the popular mode of river crossing again.

Around 30 ferrymen and boats plied between Kinnoull, on the north bank opposite Perth, and the town itself. It was common for the ferrymen to base themselves on the furthest shore, in this case opposite Perth. They named the place in a moment of faith, Bridge-end, but they had a long wait: the next bridge was not opened until 1771. The new 'red' bridge, so-called on account of the colour of the stone, was designed by John Smeaton. Its opening was of such importance that a halfpenny coin was stamped with an image of the ferryman alongside his boat to commemorate the event.

But this was all still a long way off in 1620. From then until the new bridge proudly spanned the Tay, Bridge-end emerged as one of the most important ferry crossings in Scotland, and certainly the most important in Perthshire. Private enterprise and opportunistic businessman were quick to take advantage of people's desire to cross from one side to the other. Ferrymen and their boats provided for business in a free market, and their flourishing trade did not go unnoticed.

Clearly the city fathers were not going to let such an opportunity for raising capital pass them by without taking a share. For nearly a century, the Perth town council had attempted to regulate the ferry services, mindful of the safety issues, but all too keenly aware of just how their coffers could be filled through a system of licensing. But try as they might, and although some regulations were established, the city fathers were unable to raise enough money in this way to employ an overseer, so the local ferrymen continued to enjoy a free market. The hours of service did settle down into a timetable of sorts, decided by the ferrymen responding to public demand. The ferry crossings were available daily from 5 a.m. to 10 p.m. between April and September, and from 7 a.m. to 8 p.m. during the rest of the year.

Romantic as it might have appeared, ferrying was in fact a hard life, and a career best suited to strong young men. Interestingly, in the early 1700s the average age of a ferryman in Perth was 19 years old, but it appears that as these young men realised this could be a job for life, they rarely retired at all, or refused to concede their particular trading route to others. Within a couple of generations, as fewer, new, young men were able to break into this lucrative and secure trade, the average age was much older and, consequently, the safety of the crossing was less safe. There were at least 13 ferry locations up and down the Tay in a multitude of rural areas. Those who owned the land on either side of the crossings got a slice of a very profitable business by charging the ferryman for the right to use the riverbank.

Many of the ferry services in Perthshire were remarkably well documented and illustrated. The ferry at Waulkmill is one of the few where there is still displayed an old fares table, signed by E.U. McNab, Perth District Clerk, in 1920. Each person crossing was charged 1d (a penny being worth between £1 and £1.80 today); with a bicycle, 2d; horse, 3d; a motorcar, 6d; and for each cow or beast, 2d. If there were more than a dozen beasts, half-rate would be charged.

Some of the ferries were still operating in the early 20th century, such as that at Burnbank, in order to allow the workforce of the flourishing mills at Stanley to cross over. Many ferries had their origins rooted firmly in the church, to transport parishioners across the river to attend worship on a Sunday. Although the bishops had greatly desired a bridge of some sort to be erected at Dunkeld from the thirteenth century onwards, it would be 500 years before Telford's stone bridge finally connected the south and north banks of the Tay at Dunkeld in 1809.

In the eighteenth century the ferries took a different type of passenger on board. In place of making their cattle swim, many of the farmers wished to transport their beasts with greater safety on board the ferries. The ferrymen, entrepreneurs to the tips of their calloused fingers, were swift to oblige. They built great flat-bottomed boats. These were nothing more than the original boats topped with wide platforms, and edged with a fence. The cattle would be driven on, on one side of the river, the gate would be closed, and then they would be driven off on the other side. As general prosperity increased these flat-bottomed boats were also used for horses and carts. The driver could now sit in his cart as he boarded on one side, and drive off on the other without even climbing down. Carters were more than keen to use the service and would race to a ferry crossing in order to be the first in line, and therefore first to reach potential customers if, for example, they were salesmen of cloths or groceries.

Some ferries were operated by a man with a long pole to push himself across, rather like a punt on the Cam at Cambridge. Others were modernised by securing chains to poles positioned on either side of the crossing, and the ferryman would pull the ferry across using the chain-winding mechanism, an operation which took much less effort.

Long before this type of ferry became commonplace, some much smaller ferries closer to Loch Tay, at Aberfeldy, Pittanacree and

Flat-bottomed ferry boat moored at the Logierait side of the Tay, with the Logierait Inn in the background.

The river ferry at the River Tummel, just down stream from Logierait, used to transport cattle, carriages and eventually cars. The ferryman is taking his ease on a convenient wheelbarrow.

Kenmore, were also used for transporting cattle. But these were commonly used for more illicit purposes – they provided ideal, rapid escape routes for stolen cattle. It's no wonder that criminal acts were punished adjacent to one of the most famous ferries on the Tay.

Logierait possesses today few obvious, outward signs of its importance in days gone by. The church, the old inn, and various houses gathered round an awkward corner are merely an annoyance to drivers passing through. But situated close to the confluence of both great rivers Tay and Tummel, Logierait was a vital crossing and meeting place for the most powerful of the land for around 500 years. Robert III built himself a castle, now vanished, and the duke of Atholl meted out justice there until 1748, from within 'the noblest apartment in Perthshire'. This was a Grand Hall, 70 feet long with galleries at either end, and it was also the courtroom with a convenient jail alongside. One of the most famous inmates was Rob Roy, who managed to escape and therefore avoided the hangman's noose,

Logierait in the late 19th century. The cottages appear better maintained than in 1776, when the Rev. William Gilpin, touring Scotland, noted that inside the the cottage where he stopped for some refreshment, he encountered the 'mistress of the family with several of her children beside her. The good woman was dirty, black and overgrown, and seems just like Sir John Falstaff in petticoats. It was a low, smoky hut, the door of which could hardly be entered without creeping. The thatched roof was not waterproof and the rafters were drooping with inky fluid.'

attached to a huge ash tree, 63 feet high and 40 feet wide, which stood beside the east ferry landing place. It was an ideal situation to remind the populace about the power of the laird and his rulings, as many would be able to see the unfortunate criminal hanging from the tree. In 1911, the chain-driven ferryboat was still operating at Logierait and ran parallel to the railway bridge which still exists today having been adapted for cars.

Where the River Tay widens, at least three ferries crossed over: from Lindores by Newburgh to Errol; from Newburgh to Port Allen, which is further downstream; and from Ferryfield, within the ancient settlement of Carpow, to Cairney Pier, in the grounds of Pitfour Castle. By 1845 Sir John Richardson of Pitfour had modernised the quay to accommodate steam-powered boats, and these continued just into the twentieth century. Not one ferry now exists to cross either the Tay or the Earn, or indeed any of the great rivers in Perthshire. A complete way of life has vanished, and there is nobody now living who remembers with any clarity travelling on a ferry. Of all the ferryboats that plied back and forth for many centuries, carrying both the rich and the famous, the powerful and the everyday folk, along with many thousands of cattle and sheep, not one remains in working order.

Many bridges have made it much easier now to cross these rivers, at Aberfeldy, Bridge of Earn, Perth and Dunkeld, as well as other places. The irony is, however, that nowadays bridges give you much less choice of where to transfer from one side to the other. Excepting the road bridges within Perth, for example, there exist merely two major road bridges crossing the Tay: one is two miles to the east at Friarton and the other is at Dundee.

A much easier mode of transport was gradually snaking its way across Perthshire in the mid-nineteenth century. The opportunity of railway travel indeed arrived early to the inhabitants of Perthshire. By 1848, four separate rail companies had built lines which connected at the hub, Perth. Today only a skeleton of the original network remains. Of the total of 268 miles of track at the railway's zenith in 1948, only 98 miles remain, and the number of stations has declined from 78 to 11.

The rail networks reflected the existing patterns of travel in Perthshire. From the north to the south, following the route of the A9 became a priority, as did developing the line further south from Perth

An early attempt at an integrated transport service as the tram stands at the ready to convey passengers between the train station at Inchture to the village centre.

to Edinburgh. This was made easier in 1890, when the Forth Rail Bridge opened the way for travel, dispensing with so much reliance on ferries. The east route from Perth to Dundee was one of the earliest lines, opening in 1847. But although rail links did eventually connect Perth westwards as far as Lochearnhead, with branches off to Killin, a direct route through to Oban never materialised. Such a route was really only of interest to tourists, not to trade. It still is.

The foundation stone for Perth Station was laid in 1847, but its opening had been pre-empted by the opening in 1837 of the Newtyle to Coupar Angus railway, with two carriages hauled by a steam engine. This line, like the many others which were to follow in rapid succession in the next 100 years, had a struggle to survive. The steam engine – such an innovation and pride of the embryonic railways – was an expensive item to maintain and run. Other methods of hauling the train had to be found urgently to save on fuel. Ingenuity and local expertise came to the rescue.

The story goes that a Mr McIntosh of Meigle came to the rescue. Aware of the winds which whistled across the Vale of Strathmore on

By 1922 Meigle station looked as though it had become a staunch commuter station. This line was on the Alyth branch line.

Railway staff were frequently proud of their uniforms, often complete with brass buttons bearing the railway seal. These Coupar Angus staff members cared for the station and passengers.

many days of the year, he fitted the solitary passenger carriage with masts at the corners. When the wind was in the right direction, a tarpaulin was stretched between the masts. With a good stiff breeze astern, the carriage could top speeds of 20 miles per hour. If the wind dropped, a horse would be pressed into service. In order to make sure a suitable horse was readily available, and presumably to minimise delays, the horse was either trotting behind the final passenger carriage at the rear, or aboard the rear of the train on its own dandy cart. The Seal of the Newtyle and Coupar Angus Railway Company depicts this scene in a fanciful manner.

Sail carriages were used for but a few years, and then the 'Strathmore' steam engine successfully pulled the carriages. But horse-drawn railway carriages were a popular alternative to steam for many hard-pressed fledgling railway companies struggling to make ends meet.

The trains that ran on the Newtyle to Coupar Angus line terminated at Ardler Station. But the village, which now is called Ardler, originally carried a different name from that of the station. The original name of the village was Washington, and Ardler Station differed in name from Washington village until at least the 1890s.

George Kinloch was responsible for both building the model village and naming it as Washington. He was an unusual combination of a local laird and an outspoken believer in the rights of ordinary people. After a supposedly seditious speech in Dundee on 10 November 1819, he left for France, prudently absenting himself in case of arrest. He eventually returned and stood successfully as Dundee's first elected member in the reformed Parliament of 1833. He died before his model village was built, but his son, also named George, carried on much of his father's work. To encourage the building of substantial houses, exemptions from feu duty were to be granted, for a short period. Potential householders were also to be reminded that they would have a vote in the county of Perth.

Although the original name of the village was to have been Whitehills, George Kinloch decided that Washington was a more appropriate name. It was a clear political statement, of course, as the elder George Kinloch had been a great admirer of George Washington, the first American president. Following on from this core decision, other streets variously carried on the theme. Main Street was to have been Franklin Street, after Benjamin Franklin. Other streets bore the

The seal of the Newtyle to Coupar Angus Railway appears to reassure nervous travellers that the train will complete its journey by whatever means available.

Many small communities were linked by a network of railways, such as this one at Almondbank, one of seven stops between Perth and Crieff.

This relaxed scene is at Alyth, where the Caledonian line terminated.

A late 19th-century view of St Fillans station, a scene of calm with lack of bustle, on the popular picturesque Balquhidder to Crieff route.

names of other inspirational heroes: Wallace, after William Wallace, and Cartwright Place, commemorating Major John Cartwright, a prominent Scottish radical.

The end of the nineteenth century and the early part of the twentieth was a time of mass communication not unlike texting is today. Postcards, letters and telegrams whizzed across the county alerting friends and relatives of an imminent visit. Often the visit was to be that day, or the next. Using only public transport such as rail links, it was perfectly possible to travel from Perth to Alyth, Methven to St Fillans, or Stanley to Coupar Angus in time for tea, and be back home for supper. Frequent stops at small halts added to the convenience. A railway station was, for many, not too far away.

There was the Stormont Loch platform and the Rosemount halt between Coupar Angus and Blairgowrie. Madderty, Abercairny and Innerpeffrey were all halts along the line north of Perth between the Almond Valley junction and Crieff. Indeed, the line did not stop there, but went in a circle round by Comrie, St. Fillans, Lochearnhead, Kingshouse, Strathyre, Callander, Doune and ending at Dunblane. Dunblane is the lone survivor of this link.

Many miles of railways connected Perthshire, spreading out like a cat's cradle, with Perth sitting resplendent in the centre. Perth Station in its heyday was truly an evocative sight, the epitome of Victorian imagery. A painting of the station by George Earl, completed in 1895, portrays large baskets packed with game shot on the surrounding moors, crowds of wide-skirted and extravagantly hatted ladies, and babies swathed in broderie anglaise. The railways not only inspired such painterly scenes, but also provided more prosaic income from the cattle and sheep being transported to and from market, and stock being taken to slaughter from the rich farmlands just outside the city boundaries.

Perhaps one of the most endearing rail journeys was that of the special train which ran on a dedicated line purely for transporting curlers from Blackford to the nearby loch at Carsebreck. Opened in 1851, the line was used a mere 25 times before closing in 1935.

This was to transport curlers to the loch for a Grand Match or Bonspiel between curling teams from all over Scotland. The ice must have been of considerable thickness, as the final match in 1935 attracted 2,576 curlers, with the trains presumably operating a shuttle service to transport all the competitors and spectators.

Stathtyre Station, with pride of place being given to the elaborate fountain depicting a stork. Little wonder Strathyre became a popular destination for holidays taken in parked train coaches in the 1950s.

Loch Tay station under snow. Many of the train stations were situated in picturesque areas and the station's garden and landscaping were also the pride and joy of the local station keeper.

The Hercules Garden at Blair Castle boasts a large sheet of water which was used for curling in the depths of winter.

A painting of the scene in 1898 shows gentleman players clad in stalwart tweeds, discussing tactics over much puffing of pipes, and illustrates a sense of serenity and nostalgia. Ladies are few in number, but clad also in sensible ankle-length tweed skirts and clutching their curling brooms, clearly all set for action. Although depicting a match of considerable competitiveness, there is no attempt to differentiate the teams by mode of dress. How times have changed!

CHAPTER 6

THE KING OF FISH, A CENTURY OF RASPBERRIES AND EXTINCT BEASTS

Alfred Barnard spent a happy few months in the 1880s on a travelogue with a purpose: to record all the distilleries in the United Kingdom. He published his findings in *The Whisky Distilleries of the United Kingdom* in 1886. The title does the contents of the book little justice, as his journeying was full of amusing anecdotes.

At that time, Scotland supported 129 distilleries, in contrast to four in England and 28 in Ireland. Barnard was diligent in his travelling and research, and modern-day tourists might feel a twang of envy of his ability to progress in considerable comfort and be met and entertained in a multitude of inviting hostelries, imbibing all the way.

The business of distilling had changed drastically after legislation in 1823 halved the amount of duty payable per gallon of whisky, and the more efficient and enterprising of the whisky distillers embraced this legal trade. As the illegal distillers themselves revealed, there emerged an interesting record of what were almost certainly multiple illicit operators scattered across glens, who had combined their ready access to clean streams with generations of expertise in distilling.

Many distilleries which then existed did not even survive to the end of the nineteenth century. Between Dunkeld and Pitlochry was Kilmorich, adjacent to the Tulliemet Burn at Kindallachan. This only operated for 17 years, and a further two distilleries on the banks of the Tulliemet Burn, at Milton of Tulliemet, and another below Auchnabeich, lasted but a decade or less. The only evidence left is a foundation and a stone bridge spanning the burn.

Four of the seven distilleries in Perthshire, which Barnard visited, have vanished, of which Tulliemet remains one of the most appealing. Barnard left his 'worthy landlord Mr. Fisher' (of Fishers Hotel in Pitlochry, which still exists) and was driven in a trap drawn by a 'very smart horse', past the Moulin Hotel. Although he pointed out that it was usual for most travellers to regain their strength there with a glass or so of Atholl Brose, 'a celebrated local compound of whisky and honey', he much preferred whisky neat.

He waxed eloquent about the scenery as they approached the Tulliemet Distillery, and indeed must have been viewing it in Elysian conditions. For although the distillery was apparently in a 'somewhat desolate' position in the centre of some farm lands resembling a collection of ramshackle farm buildings, no production was taking place as the weather was 'too hot for malting'.

Water trickled down from the Auchnagie Hills to concoct this elixir, which was sold simply as a 'Highland Malt'. The production of 19,000 gallons was quite modest, compared with most of the other local distilleries he visited, although he did point out that this production would rise to 24,000 gallons. But he gained the impression that no-one was too worried about a possible increased workload with increased production. The distillery employed just one excise man, 'who informed us that he leads quite a pastoral life here, and spends his summer days in his garden and little farmyard'.

The distillery was short-lived after this visit, and the business of the then owner, given as a Mr P. Dawson, was dissolved. John Dewar, who was building up his whisky business into the empire it became in the twentieth and twenty-first centuries, then took on the Tulliemet lease. This was the very first distillery he took over and the whisky was taken down to the railway station at Ballinluig by horse and cart. This arrangement only survived until 1896, when Dewar found that his business was more cost-effective if based in a brand new distillery close to Aberfeldy.

The duke of Atholl decided to offer the Tulliemet lease on the open market, but the whisky industry was changing rapidly, and no one accepted the offer. So ended centuries of whisky production in the Tulliemet area. Tulliemet was also home to a most ingenious system for concealing the still from the prying, and eagle-eyed excisemen. Local entrepreneur Alex Cameron applied more imagination than many to his secrets. Behind his house at Tomnald, by the Broom Burn he, or his elders, had dug out a dam for steeping the barley. As this was difficult to conceal, the dam was effectively covered over with planks upon which were placed divots of turf, which was grazed by sheep. It must have been a cunning and an effective ruse.

In the area stretching eastwards from Ballinluig to Dowally there were at least six distilleries, mainly small concerns situated near farms. East Haugh of Ballyoukan, now a private house, was once the site of a distillery. The iron bars on the back of the house suggest it might have been the storage warehouse, according to Jane Banner in her book *The Braes of Tulliemet*. She found that 'although records of 1798 show that John Scott had this distillery, it then changed hands four times before its closure in 1852'. By this time the proprietor, Charles Duff and Co., owned another distillery on the other side of the River Tay at Tomdachoil.

Two other distilleries in the area were short-lived. One at Pitcastle had three owners until vanishing from the records.

Alfred Barnard was warming to his enjoyment of Perthshire by the time he reached the Ballechin Distillery.

Travelling in an open carriage is exceedingly pleasant. There is more freedom about it than the railway, for you are your own master, free to hurry or dawdle as you please. Sometimes you may want to reach your destination quickly. At other times you may wish to enjoy the country; to pause here and there, and watch the far seeing panorama. Yesterday at Aberfeldy, and today at Pitlochry, Ballinluig and Ballechin, moving through such enchanting scenery, we have felt that our locomotion could not be too slow, and at several nooks and places on the sides we would fain have pitched our tent, and dwelt there a while to enjoy the rich treasures of beauty spread before us. We are passing through a district rich in traditions and legendary lore, and abounding in scenes of enthralling interest. As we drive through the parish of Logierait, our worthy coachman, who knows the object of our visit, reminds us that we are in the heart of a district famous from a most remote period for the distillation of whisky. The burns, or small streams, which rise in the peat mosses and bog of Ballechin moor, under the shade of the Fergan range of hills, fall into the Tay and are associated at every secluded bend and shady corner with the smuggling bothy, where illicit distillation was carried on extensively in olden times.

The story of the smugglers of local, illicit whisky was the stuff of legend. Barnard proceeds to spin the tale of one of the last known smugglers, a Mr Stewart, whose audacity became famous. One night

Stewart was rowing down river to Perth from Strathtay, to deliver a few barrels of whisky, having alerted his accomplices closer to the town of his arrival, which happened to be at Halloween. Perhaps this date was a happy embellishment.

As the smuggling Stewart was rowing his booty to the arranged meeting point, he noticed at the very last minute that in place of his friends were the men from the excise waiting for him. Desperately he attempted to row single-handedly away, but the excisemen seized an empty boat, and rowed after him, eventually closing the gap. Stewart thought it prudent to show signs of surrender, and seizing an oar from the excise men, invited them to scramble onto his boat. But, of course, it was a trick, and Stewart flung the seized oar onto his boat, leaving the other boat with a single oar with which to limp home. Stewart landed his barrels at another hidden place and disaster was averted. As, indeed, it continued to be for a few more years.

His swansong was a load of barrels which he conveyed to Leith in Edinburgh in a canopied cart, inside which was a 'patient' with an infectious disease. Thus he managed to evade any curious excisemen and land his load safely.

Ballechin Distillery was established in 1810, but by the time Barnard visited the site, it had been owned since 1875 by Messrs. Robertson and Sons. Barnard describes it as being built in an L-shape into the side of the hill, the water being supplied by a weird place called Collin's Hollow which he then went on to praise, as this particular water supply must have been so pure that the steam boiler showed not the slightest encrustation.

So carried away was Barnard by the beauty of the scene, that he had to drag himself reluctantly back to his job in hand, the description of the distillery, the workings of which he found very old fashioned and idiosyncratic. Much of the machinery was owed to the inventiveness of the owner, but it was the distillery worm itself which he declared was the most ancient he had set eyes upon in his tour, and was a 'regular smugglers worm, laid in a vessel and fed from the overflow of the burn'. Finally, he observed also that the peat used did not come from close by, this being almost inaccessible, but instead from the Orkneys and Inverness-shire.

Curiously, the water from the 'weird place' has now vanished. The water table has changed in the intervening years, but as for the origins of the stream which supplied the Ballechin Distillery, not a

Waterfalls such these, the Middle Falls at Moness near Aberfeldy, demonstrate the superfluity of fast flowing water, much used for distilling.

trace is to be found. The remains of the corrugated roofed buildings are adjacent to the road, and in use by a local joiner.

'We got off the train at Grantully Station,' declared Barnard, 'where we hired a vehicle at the village inn, and drove to the distillery, 3 miles distant. A prettier drive can hardly be conceived in summertime, the road for the most part of the way being carried through plantations and past the fine old Castle of Grandtully, immortalized by Sir Walter Scott.'

He was much amused by the loquacious driver, the grandson of one of the smugglers, who recounted the following story.

The original distillery was situated in a farmhouse perched on top of the hill. Beneath a farmhouse kitchen was a spacious cave, accessed through what appeared to be a dried-up river-bed, which in turn was disguised by stones and rocks, therefore allowing a very small trickle of water to enter the cave. Incredibly the illegal still was then connected down a flue about 70 yards from where they had their furnaces. The entire operation was completely concealed, and the farmhouse operated as the base for the farmer tilling his land, as well as a judicious lookout position for approaching excisemen. But eventually there was a dispute between the illicit distillers, and one of the smugglers tipped off the excisemen. In the raid that followed, both the smugglers managed to escape, eventually finding their way to America. The story goes that 10 years later they repented and returned to the area.

Grandtully was, in the 1880s, the smallest distillery in the United Kingdom, and was perceived to be the most 'primitive workings we have ever seen', and all the work was carried out by the young manager, Donald Thompson.

Upon tasting the whisky, Barnard found it very delicate in flavour and smooth, which was a rare comment for him. He did not appear to be alone in his appreciation. In fact, the proprietor, Sir Douglas Stewart, was employing architects to draw up plans to enlarge the distillery, and install modern and up-to-date equipment to increase production. But young Mr Thompson was reluctant to enter into partnership with Sir Douglas Stewart for some unknown reason, and the plans were shelved.

This could have been a less than wise decision by Thompson.

Grandtully Distillery was no longer in production by 1900, a mere 14 years after Barnard visited.

Not far distant, and 250 years before, the brewers – in the plural – of Logierait were admonished by the Presbytery: 'on May 22, 1641 it was ordained that brewers must not sell ale or give drink on the Sabbath before the sermon finishes and the congregation dismissed. The Brewers of the Towne of Logierait held up their hands in pledge'.

Logierait Inn flourishes today, serving whisky from many of the famous Perthshire distillers, such as John Dewar, and dishing up salmon for which the Tay is famous. Fresh river salmon today is an expensive luxury, both for fishermen to try their luck, as well as customers. It was not always so.

Salmon fishing was an extra income for many farm workers, notably the weavers from Scone, who supplemented their winter wages by fishing from January until the close of the season in August. In addition to weaving, their dexterous skills were applied to constructing nets for fishing. But, although salmon was plentiful and netted in abundance, this very abundance made it an easily available and cheap food for both farm workers and those employees of the landed estates. Both farm workers and estate employers frequently referred to a common clause in their contacts of employments, whereby a restriction on the number of days' salmon would be part of their diet. There are many instances of strongly worded complaints of a daily diet of salmon.

This was mainly due, of course, not only the prevalence of salmon, but also to the lack of effective preservation methods of the fish. But the arrival of the train system to London in the mid-nineteenth century opened up many possibilities. Salmon were parboiled, chopped up into small enough pieces to be packed into barrels, covered with vinegar and then sent to London and the lucrative markets of the south. Later, as the trains covered the distance with much greater speed, the fish was packed in ice and delivered fresh to the market.

Ice houses were then built close to the largest of the fishing stations on the Tay. Built into the hill, barrel-shaped with stone vaulting and often with scarcely enough space to stand upright, the ice houses were of sturdy construction. Usually with large double entrance doors, and facing north to minimise the heating effect of the sun, they were packed with ice brought in by sea from the Baltic each year. An early attempt at preservation by freezing, they transformed the fortunes of the salmon fishing businesses up and down the Tay, as fresh salmon was clearly a much more attractive option than fish preserved in vinegar. Very few of these ice houses survive today.

Salmon netting was once a common sight on the lower reaches of the Tay from Perth to Dundee, but had vanished by the end of the twentieth century.

For salmon netters, this was a seasonal job, lasting through the summer months, and bothies were built specially built for their use.

The Tay Valley viewed from Grandtully, close to the small distillery viewed by Alfred Barnard as he toured the United Kingdom in 1885 visiting and comprehensively recording every distillery in the land.

These were situated within ten metres or so from the high water mark of the river. The vast majority of bothies, which can still be seen today from the river today, have no road access.

Little is documented about the bothies. The ruins of some which date to the early nineteenth century can still be found. Occasionally a more modern, early 20th century house sits within a stone's throw of a ruined bothy. As netting salmon on the river has ceased, and the only fishing for salmon now is by rod and line, there is not one bothy which is still used for its original purpose. The reason that bothies occupied a position so close to the river's edge was so that the salmon netters could waste little time travelling. As netting could only be carried out during times of high tides, and these, of course fluctuated over both day and night, the netters were required to work during hours of light and darkness. Furthermore, salmon netting could only be undertaken from Monday early mornings to Saturday evenings, the Sabbath being deemed a rest day for both men and fish.

If the catches during successive seasons were consistently good, then an investment would be made by banking up the river edge with stone walling, so that the casting of the net would be easier, faster and enable nets to be launched more often, leading to more fish being caught.

While improvements were made to the bothies over the years, little improvements were required either to the design of the boats and the methods of casting the nets.

These salmon boats, known as cobles, were constructed to a design unchanged since the 16th century. Cobles, still used on the great fishing rivers are, indeed, still constructed and so well developed for their purpose, that their design has shown no need for modern modifications – apart from the addition of an engine to replace oars. When cobles overturn, they can be immediately righted, emptied out and put straight back to use again. Their elegant shape belies their workhorse capabilities. The flat panel at the stern of the boat was used for the nets.

Many of the netters, as it was a seasonal job, lived on the banks of the Tay because they required rapid access to the river day and night. Some bothies have been adapted for other uses. They can still be spotted, dotted along both banks of the Tay between Perth and Dundee, and built so close to the river's edge that it looks as though you could fish for your supper from the front window.

Most are now ruinous, but some are relatively new, built at least since World War II. Occasionally one of the ruinous ones still contains the remains of single beds, but arranged in pairs, head to foot.

The origins of many of these small fishing bothies are not well documented, having been of little importance to the estates upon which they were built. Generally, the older, ruinous ones were probably built at the end of the nineteenth century and now are rarely to be found. Others would have been constructed in a later fluctuating but continuous programme of building.

Why these bothies were built in such isolated locations owed little to chance, but a great deal to the ability of the fishermen to launch nets from that location, and the success-rate of their catch. If the catch-rate over the years was good, then the bank was well built up so that the boats could be easily launched and the men could walk along the shore and haul in the salmon. When the bothy lapsed into a poor condition, and the catching was still good, then the salmon-fishing company would build another. If, on the other hand, the fishing deteriorated, then the bothy was unceremoniously abandoned, and fishing was taken further up or down stream. On the Tay, many abandoned elderly bothies can be seen and right along the north bank between Perth and Dundee. One of the last to be built, which was never really successful owing to the building of the Friarton Bridge almost overhead, can be seen just east of Perth, north of junction 10 on the M90.

The season ran from the first week in February until the end of August, and the fishing hours were from 6 a.m. on Monday to 6 p.m. on Saturday. The men who worked in these bothies often came from generations of the same families – brothers, sons and fathers working together. After the fishing finished, there was other casual seasonal work to turn to, such as harvesting. The men would leave home on a Sunday night, carrying their food for the week and wend their way down to their bothy. Once there, they stuck to a system of five hours working, seven hours off. Most bothies had at least one or two fireplaces, set into the gable-end walls, and they would be divided into at least two rooms. Often the centre section, opposite the front door, was an open space with open beams at least a couple of metres off the floor where clothes and boots could be dried. Later bothies had their fireplaces set into the inner walls of each room, the warmth from the flues radiating into this central area for drying clothes. Few, if any, of the older bothies had electricity, being in such an isolated position, and this was true even of bothies in use well after World War II.

Over the years the fishing bothies became more civilised, and cooking facilities improved, but the method of net fishing for salmon, still occasionally carried out on the coast, changed hardly at all. The net was piled onto the boat which then swept out in an arc, while the other shore-based fisherman dragged his end of the net along the shore, in line with the boat. The two ends were then winched together, the fish being trapped in the net bag which was created. The fish were killed, weighed and put into the cold store. In the old days, the fish would be collected each day by a boat going up and down the river and taken to a central point where they would be kept in an ice house, and sent off to the market by train from Perth. Until just before the end of their usefulness in the 1990s, the bothies had vehicle access and the fish were collected by road.

Salmon fishing cobles, similar to this one, were used for netting for hundreds of years.

At Newton, Blairgowrie, the seat of the Macphersons of Cluny, records show that salmon were netted on the Ericht from artificial stone projections, called croys, which created shelter for the salmon. From these stone projections, great nets were launched to capture the fish. In 1805, 364 fish were trapped in one single haul of the net. Little surprise that salmon so easily trapped should be an almost daily and inexpensive meal for agricultural workers in the late eighteenth and early nineteenth century. Employers would have preferred to feed their workers as often as possible on such a cheap commodity.

As the textile mills were constructed on the Ericht during the middle of the nineteenth century, with their system of lades, diversions of water and eventually much effluent and noxious chemicals from the weaving and dyeing processes, the salmon were drastically reduced in number, and the great netting days on the Ericht came to an end.

Innovation was needed, therefore, to find other products from Perthshire's land and water, and new markets from which to sell them.

Much of the land proved excellent for crops, such as potatoes, and seed potatoes formed an ever-increasing export from many areas of Perthshire, filling the local goods trains that criss-crossed the counties. The Dundee, Perth and London Shipping Co., founded in 1826, then picked up the sacks of seed potatoes and dispatched them to areas such as Lincolnshire, which were very successful in growing good potato crops.

As potatoes became such an important crop in Perthshire, production became large-scale, and the many less common varieties were in danger of being lost.

However, an attempt to save at least some of the old varieties, which would have been grown in small gardens all over Perthshire, was launched in the 1970s and 1980s by Donald Maclean of Dornock Farm near Crieff. He encouraged with missionary zeal the growing of 'lost' varieties of potatoes, many of which had stories which he feared were disappearing, and which he expounded with fervour. Within what he referred to as his 'museum field', he grew dozens of different varieties, from which he sold seed potatoes in order to keep the varieties alive.

'These are lumpers,' he pointed out to me in 1990. 'They are the ones which were grown in Ireland and caused the death of about two million Irish people in the famine. Can't you see the tears of remorse coming from them? It was all because of these tatties and their susceptibility to blight that New York has a St Patrick's Day parade.'

'They were not mentioned in the pulpit, you see,' he said, expounding his own theory of the development of the crop, 'because they had to be picked out of the ground, so they were dirty things. But they made the Industrial Revolution possible, a cheap way of feeding the masses. I have a love-hate relationship with them.'

He loved his potatoes, and his knowledge was such that letters addressed to him simply as 'Potato Man, Scotland' generally arrived safe and sound. But it was his search for every different type of use for them that drew him in his final years to encourage the development of potato starch to be used as a plastic-like fabric to replace the plague of the plastic bag, as it is genuinely biodegradable. As this was in the 1980s, he was truly ahead of his time. His museum of potatoes has vanished, but his approach to preserving old varieties and encouraging the growth of a much wider variety of potatoes than those usually on offer has taken root, so to speak. He would be pleased to see that many more retailers now offer six or more varieties, although but a fraction of the wide number of varieties once grown.

Perhaps the crop most associated with Perthshire, though, is raspberries. Raspberries and strawberries were grown only for home consumption until the 1880s when an enterprising local named Martin

Moran, who lived at the Smiddy Brae in Old Rattray, had the idea of growing raspberries on a small commercial scale, to be sent to the Glasgow market by train. That most of the fruit grown in the area was used locally was entirely understandable: the season was fairly short, the fruit was highly perishable and it probably never occurred to anyone locally that a business could be created from this small red fruit.

J.M. Hodge, a great-grandfather of the present solicitor practising in Blairgowrie, was one of the first to realise that this fruit could be propagated with ease. Raspberry plants will subdivide themselves and, given the correct conditions and climate, spread in almost epidemic proportions. Blairgowrie and the surrounding area naturally provide near-perfect conditions in terms of soil, and, in a good year, equally excellent conditions in terms of climate.

Martin Moran's rasps, growing in the one-acre field behind Rattray School, produced an astonishing six tons of fruit, worth from £31, which equated to around 75 per cent of an entire annual agricultural wage. But the fluctuations were large, because if the weather conditions were cold and raining when the fruits were ripening, the crop would perish too rapidly to make it saleable even the following day. So what could be done with the raspberries even if they were less than perfect, owing to inclement weather conditions? The answer lay in transforming and effectively adding value and longer life to this highly perishable fruit in one fell swoop, in preserving it in one of the least perishable methods then on offer: as jam. But this could only ever have been a small-scale operation in Blairgowrie.

At this point, J.M. Hodge formed the Blairgowrie and Rattray Fruitgrowers Association in 1895, and the raspberries were picked, packed into barrels and sent to Hartley's, major jam-makers in the United Kingdom and based in Liverpool. All this was made possible because of the arrival of the railway in Blairgowrie in 1855. The fruit was preserved by the addition of sulphur, which rendered the fruit yellow by effectively stripping out the scarlet colour. The natural colour was restored, however, when the fruit was boiled for jam. There had been a small, local jam factory situated behind Adamson's shop in the High Street, but the ability to send large quantities south to a factory meant that the small-scale growing of raspberries could now be dramatically increased. The market for the crop was confidently assured.

It was the necessity of obtaining a large workforce for these large fields of raspberries which transformed Blairgowrie from a sleepy market town into a busy, semi-industrial zone for a couple of months of the year. The main problem was that the local area simply could not produce the pickers in the numbers required by trying to bring them in on a daily commuting basis, being too far from the major towns of Dundee and Perth to transport them quickly enough. Picking was in the middle of summer, and, if necessary, pickers would be out in the fields for long hours of daylight. The crop required hundreds of pickers, and as a few more local entrepreneurs rented land and produced crops and the acreage of raspberries increased, pickers required to be housed for those vital couple of months of the year, and the closer to the fields the better. James McDonald of Welton Farm, just southeast of the town, was the first to erect prefabricated huts for the workers.

In 1905 the area around Essendy became known as 'Tin City' as dozens of neat, corrugated iron sheds sprang up, and were fitted out with beds, dormitory-style. To house a thousand or so workers was quite an undertaking. There were 48 dormitories, each with 20 beds to accommodate 960 pickers. To service this small village there were two kitchens and three spacious dining rooms capable of seating 1,000. One room became a writing room in the evenings. Another was transformed into an entertainment area with a piano. There were sheds for washing and drying clothes, shops, stationers and a post office, effectively creating a self-contained village. There was a matron and supervisor, a 'cleansing' officer to oversee the sanatorium, and 30 domestic staff to cook and clean. It was a forerunner of a Butlin's holiday camp, complete with concerts on week nights and religious services on Sundays, but with work replacing leisure hours.

In the years prior to World War I, the pickers were mostly local young women, drawn from waitresses, servants, shop assistants, factory workers, students and school pupils. But as the demand for pickers rose and the work requirement was packed into such a short season, the search for pickers stretched as far as Glasgow and Dundee, from where whole families flocked for this alternative, and affordable, summer holiday. Travellers had always appeared in the area around that time as well, and they set up camp close to the fields. Both the numbers of pickers and the fact that they were a captive audience, so to speak, meant that the area also attracted missionaries.

Marlie (or Marlee) House sitting on the loch of the same name became the centre of the great soft fruit growing area surrounding Blairgowrie.

The Rev. George Brown of Bendochy provided the impetus to build a 'Tin Kirk' from which he and others preached to the hundreds who gathered there.

Further to the west, at Dowally, just a few miles north of Dunkeld off the A9, was quite a different celebration associated with fruit – and this might have included raspberries as well as other home-grown fruit. This was the annual 'japping market', named after the old Scots word 'jap', or 'jaup', meaning to splash with water. According to the *Statistical Account of Scotland* in 1791: 'The herds (farm labourers) in the course of the day, arranged themselves on each side of the burn of Dowally; on a signal given, they beat the water one against the other with sticks, till one of the competing teams conceded defeat. The vanquished then left the market, and the victors had the exclusive honour of treating the lasses to fruit, and of enjoying their society at the ball.' It is interesting to note that as this market ceased around 1743, and no records can be found of this type of fun later, it may well have been almost exclusive to Dowally.

Another curious custom took place at Cargill, involving the pretty, yellow daisy-like flower, the innocuous *Chrysanthemum segetum*, most commonly called the Corn Marigold. It used to grow on wild, disturbed ground and in cornfields, and would seed very easily, but it is rarely to be seen now. It was, and sometime still is, known by a variety of names, such as Bile Bhuidhe, Bile-bhuidhe, Dithean-oir, Manelet, Neoinean or Yellow Gowan or Goul, Gule. It was the last two names which gave rise to the custom of 'goolriding, a 'gool' being the Corn Marigold.

The *Statistical Account of Scotland* in 1795 records that 'An old custom takes place in this parish (Cargill) called Goolriding . . . imposing a fine of 3 shillings and 4 pennies (about £15 today) or a wedder (castrated male sheep) on the tenants for every stock of gool found growing among their corns at a particular day, and certain persons, styled 'goolriders' were appointed to ride through the fields and search for gools and carry the law into execution, though the fine of a wedder sheep is now commuted and reduced to one penny sterling. The practice of goolriding is still kept up and the fine rigidly exacted.' This custom look place on the Barony of Stobhall, and provides an insight into just how far the landowner would go in order to maintain the cleanliness of his crops, and extract maximum return from the harvest.

But there were also days purely devoted to celebrations in rural areas of Perthshire, and one of these, which encompassed a general feast, was held on the first day of May, the Beltane Ceremony. Thomas Pennant, wrote in 1772 about the Beltane Ceremony as observed in Perthshire.

On the first day of May, the herdsmen of every village hold their Bel-tein, a rural sacrifice. They cut a square trench on the ground, leaving the turf in the middle; on that they make a fire of wood, on which they dress a large caudle of eggs, butter oatmeal and milk; and bring, besides the ingredients of the caudle, plenty of beer and whisky; for each of the company must contribute something. The

Taken in 1910, the two ladies dressed in their Sunday best are waiting at Rosemount Station on the Blairgowrie line. By this time the area was benefiting from the burgeoning soft fruit industry.

rites begin by spilling some of the caudle upon the ground by way of libation; on that, everyone takes a cake of oatmeal, on which are raised some nine square knobs, each dedicated to some particular being, the supposed preserver of their flocks and herds; and to some particular animal the supposed destroyer of them; each person then turns his face to the fire, breaks off a knob and flinging it over his shoulder says, 'This I give to thee, preserve thou my horses; this to thee preserve thou my sheep' and so on. After that they use the same ceremony to the noxious animals; 'This I give to thee o fox, spare thou my lambs; this to thee o hooded crow; to thee o eagle.' When the ceremony is over, they dine on the caudle; and after the feast is finished, what is left is hid by two persons deputed for that purpose; but on the next Sunday they re-assemble and finish the reliques of the first entertainment.

Large country houses were built purely for pleasure, to accommodate house guests who would enjoy shooting on the acres of high moorland.

By the mid-nineteenth century, the era of recreation in Perthshire was commencing. Prince Albert, husband of Queen Victoria, was an avid hunter. By the time he arrived in the Highlands the game which he shot was confined to birds and deer, but it had certainly not always been so. Just over a century before, in 1743, the last wolf may have been killed near Findhorn, Moray, amid an outcry that it had killed two children, but as ever with such an emotive issue, others have taken a different view. Among them is Ian Nimmo, former editor of the *Edinburgh Evening News*, who spent part of his childhood between Dunkeld and Blair Atholl, an area with its own fair share of 'last wolf' traditions. It was said to be on the wooded slopes somewhere on the Atholl lands that Mary, Queen of Scots, came, with 2,000 Highland beaters, for what may have been the biggest deer hunt ever in Scotland. The haul included five wolves as well. Nimmo recalls a tale from his childhood, 'that the last wolf had been killed on Craig Vinean, at the back of Dunkeld'. Highland Perthshire was certainly once widely populated by wolves. As agriculture advanced and stock had to be protected, the wolf was hunted out, as so many accounts, such as Ian Nimmo's, suggest. But there are many descriptive passages of where wolves roamed at will. Perhaps, feared as they were, some exaggeration might have also crept into these accounts.

Rannoch and Strathearn are mentioned as being certainly the land of wolves, but contemporary accounts of the fifteenth, sixteenth and seventeenth centuries lead us to believe that vast tracts of Perthshire were positively infested with wolves, according to John Taylor, the self-styled 'Water Poet' who in 1618 travelled on foot from London to Edinburgh. He then proceeded to Braemar, most probably travelling through or skirting the northern parts of Perthshire, and reported: 'I was in the space of twelve days before I saw either house, cornfield, or habitation of any creature, but deer, wild horses, Wolves and such like creatures, which made me doubt that I should ever see a house again.'

In 1528 the Earl of Atholl entertained the king with a great hunt which lasted three days. Scores of stags and hinds, wild cats, roe deer and wolves were slaughtered. Almost two decades earlier, in around 1509, a Caithness clergyman had journeyed south to meet King Henry VIII on his accession to the throne, and answered the king's query as to why the Highlanders were nicknamed 'redshanks'. Because they roamed, winter and summer, bare-legged, hunting for red deer, foxes, badgers and wolves, came the answer.

Wolves roamed over many areas of Perthshire until the late 17th century. Although much feared and the subject of many tales, no certain evidence exists of wolves attacking people.

Such were their numbers, that the Spittal of Glenshee was established as a place of shelter from the numbers of wolves which predated on the farmed sheep and cattle.

Blair Atholl, Struan and Strathearn among other places were once the haunt of wolves, when the area was smothered in trees. Much of the forest has vanished, as well as the wolves, who were hunted to extinction around the beginning of the eighteenth century, and had been the cause of many coffins being covered with large stone slabs, to prevent the remains of the deceased being dug up and consumed by wolves.

Customs such as these, which originated far beyond living memory, are mirrored in the extinct animals which roamed the land. Some survive in folk memories and a few in place names, but others are known of only by the discovery of their bones.

The beaver was once widespread in the waters of Perthshire,

The European Beaver became extinct in Scotland around 500 years ago, having been hunted for its fur and salicylic acid within its glands.

both in the large lochs but also up the smaller burns where their engineering often created new landscapes. The beaver is often thought of as going to extinction primarily for its pelt, which was of considerable value, and was traded down to London. However, the curative powers of the beaver also are linked to the modern pharmaceutical weapon of aspirin. Most valuable of all were their castoreum glands. Due to the willow bark that beavers eat, salicylic acid (similar to and with many of the properties of modern-day aspirin) accumulates in the glands. During the Middle Ages these glands were a precious medicine and therefore highly sought. Extinct as the wild, indigenous Scots beavers have been for around 500 years, this lowly, harmless small animal has been of great historical importance to generations of Scots, and Perthshire certainly was included in this category. Beavers were slaughtered in their thousands for their pelts as well as for their glands. They were the very height of fashion for about 200 years. When James VI and I arrived in London from north of the Border, following the death of Elizabeth I in 1603, he had ordered 20 beaver hats, 17 of them to be black, lined with taffeta, trimmed with black bands and feathers, as well as a black riding hat, embroidered in gold and silver trimmed with feather plumes. It was outrageously extravagant, as the beaver hats alone cost twenty times more than the woollen equivalent. An up-and-coming tradesman in William Fenner's *The Country Commonwealth* (1616) was advised: 'Your four shilling Dutch felt hat shall be converted to a three pound beaver.' In 1861, Prince Albert arrived at the opening of the Great Exhibition wearing a silk hat. In a tilting of the royal headgear, he demonstrated that the previously impossible task of constructing a silk-covered hat on a muslin base was solved. The beaver was never in such demand again. But it was far too late to save the native beavers in Perthshire, and indeed in Scotland. There is no definite date on which they had become extinct in Perthshire, but just to the east of Blairgowrie, on the A926 road leading to Alyth, is a habitation named on old maps as Beavershire, close to North Littleton. On the western side of Blairgowrie, at the Loch of Marlee, a complete beaver skeleton was uncovered during drainage operations, and the bones were donated to the Society of Antiquities of Scotland by Dr William Farquharson of Invercauld, on 16 December 1788. The remains of this Perthshire beaver now reside in the Perth Museum.

Another creature long extinct in Perthshire is the wild boar, ancient ancestor of the domestic pig. Hunting for boar was a far greater diversion than the foxhunt or deer stalking. The wild forests of Perthshire held populations of boar as late as the fifteenth century. Every bit of a wild boar was of use – not just the flesh but the hide and bones. There was a Crieff saying that a family could utilise 'everything but the grunt' of a slaughtered wild boar. From the 1791–99 *Statistical Account of Scotland* is a reference to places on the western edges of Beinn a'Ghlo called 'Carn-torey' which might well have been a corruption of the Gaelic word 'tuirc' meaning boar. Several landowners have now brought boar back, but enclosed behind strong fences. A boar is at its happiest snuffling through the woodlands in which Perthshire is still so rich, and as they flourish, they give living proof that they did and could thrive exceedingly well.

The auroch, the animal from which domesticated cattle are descended, also prospered deep in the glades of pre-farming Perthshire. They seem to have become extinct in the Dark Ages, after the Romans had left their line of fortifications, and before the rise of a

Boar hunting was enjoyed by late medieval nobles, reflected in many names in Perthshire.

united Scottish kingdom. Similar in character to the wild, white cattle that survive in parkland such as Chillingham in Northumberland, they are barely recognisable as cousins of farm cattle. These were highly aggressive creatures and far more dangerous to man than many other now extinct fauna. In the 1770s, while dredging the small loch of the Cuilc close to the modern-day Pitlochry golf course, farmers scooped out deposits of lime and were surprised to find the preserved skulls of four giant oxen, *Uri (Bos primigenius)*.

And as for bears, we have no knowledge, again, of how long ago Perthshire was home to brown bears. There are no records of them other than some passing praise in Latin texts for the size and ferocity of Caledonian bears shipped to entertain the crowds at the Coliseum in Rome. Bears are part of our shared cultural memory, but it is odd how they are regarded either as loveable teddies or as man-eating monsters. Both are untrue. The European brown bear is shy of human contact. They are omnivorous, and would have been content fishing in Perthshire's waters and eating juniper or blackberry.

A huge creature now lost to the historical record and only known from a few skeleton finds is the elk or moose. They survive in Scandinavia, but their Scottish relatives must have been hunted down by Mesolithic inhabitants. An elk is the largest of the living deer, so it represented both a relatively easy kill plus a huge feast of flesh. An elk antler from Methven is preserved within the Perth Museum and Art Gallery, a sorry reminder of another lost animal.

The hirsute feral goats, roaming wild in Scotland, are now a rare sight, except on land owned by the National Trust for Scotland, and on various islands. This is a recent development as goats were once an intrinsic part of the Scottish landscape. The arrival of enclosures during the 18th century effectively excluded roaming animals and goats were left to forage on higher less fertile ground. They probably arrived here with the Neolithic peoples between 4000 and 2000 BC, and spread around Scotland. Their distinctive curved horns were fashioned into spoons and cooking utensils, and the soft, wavy, goat hair was ideal for making the customary sporrans sported by Scottish soldiers for generations.

Goats were most likely to have been as common before the clearances as today's quantities of sheep; and sheep and goats added together would vastly outnumber cattle. Dr Johnson in *A Journey to the Western Islands of Scotland* (1775) gave the stock of a tacksman in the Highlands on the mainland as: '100 sheep, as many goats, 12 milk cows and 28 beeves (beef cattle) ready for the drovers.'

Early in the eighteenth century, the material woven into tartan was often taken from goats or goat-like sheep, the Hebridean breeds, for example. Their distinctive, coarse hair was plucked rather than shorn, so originally all cloth was black, brown or white. In the seventeenth and eighteenth centuries, the hair was also used in the manufacture of wigs for export. During the clearance of people from the land in the late eighteenth and early nineteenth centuries, many goats escaped and became feral. Today there are reckoned to be a maximum of 4,000 feral goats living in around 141 small herds in Scotland, most groups isolated from one another. Many live on islands, but there are some herds running in isolated pockets, such as the hills northwest of Dunkeld. A far cry from the days when most crofters and farmers possessed just as many goats as sheep or cattle, when goats were nicknamed 'poor man's cattle'.

CHAPTER 7

HUNDREDS OF SCHOOLS, HIGH IDEALS AND HIGH CHURCHMEN

A trawl through the three Statistical Accounts of Scotland from the 'Old' one of 1791 to 1799 right up to the third one of the early 1950s, reveals an astounding number of schools in Perthshire, even though many of the very early ones were merely one-teacher dame schools with perhaps doubtful educational results. School building blossomed following the Education Act of 1872, which brought in compulsory education for all children aged between 5 and 13, although fees still had to be paid until 1890.

By 2010, there are 76 state primary schools listed in Perthshire. Although it's not possible to give an exact figure as to how many existed in 1901 there must have been, at the very least, 100.

Perthshire's population in 1901 was 123,283 and in 2001 was 134,949. The greatest change was in the population of Perth, which increased from nearly 30,000 to around 42,500. A list of all schools in 1901 makes it possible to pinpoint many, especially in rural areas, which have vanished over the last century. This is understandable with rural people moving to the city. The improvements in roads and public transport, of course, have played the most significant part in this decimation of the small village school.

Rural schools to which children could walk have totally vanished. The following figures, taken from records in 1901, tellingly illustrate the spread of small schools. For example, under the Kenmore Education Board were listed Ardeonaig, Ardtalnaig, Fearnan, Kiltyrie and Lawers. In all these schools, places existed for 449 children, of which the average attendance was 210 children. Today only a primary school at Kenmore still exists.

At Fowlis Wester there was Balgowan public school, Fowlis public school and Buchanty, together offering places for 265, of which the average attending was 156. None of these three exists today.

Where a single school exists today in Alyth, once there were three: a public (state) school with 311 pupils, an Episcopal one with 101, and a Church of Scotland school with 282 enrolled.

At Weem there were two: the Weem school which offered 64 places, and the Strathtay Stewart's School which had places available for 100 pupils. From its hill-top situation, Strathtay Stewart's was to become a school of great significance in the annals of Scottish education. Its origins might appear no different from the founding of other well-known Edinburgh fee-paying institutions: a typical tale of a local Scots lad from a modest background who made a fortune and founded a school. In fact, the first Daniel Stewart's school began life at an elevation of some 900 feet up a glen overlooking Strathtay, but the Edinburgh establishment only sprang to life after Daniel Stewart's death in 1846.

Daniel Stewart was a son of the croft, born in Wester Tober-an-donich ('Well of Sunday') in 1741, high up on the steep ridge overlooking the Tay, and close to the spot where his school was eventually founded. His parents came from the area. His mother, a Macfarlane, was born in the parish of Logierait, and his father was born in Dull. Their croft was on the inhospitable uplands, south-facing but windswept, and the steep slopes saw the skim of soil washed down to the Tay. The then duke of Atholl, on whose land the Stewart's croft lay, was quoted as saying that half his soil was now at the mouth of the Tay, east of Dundee.

This might have been an exaggeration, but the truth of the matter was that the croft sat upon land from which it was difficult to wrestle a livelihood. Daniel Stewart decided early in his life to seek a living elsewhere, for he next emerges in Edinburgh as an apprentice wig-maker, one of the most lucrative of trades in the 1760s, as wigs were worn by a substantial number of men and women. In fact wig-making and wearing was at its height, and it could well have been then that Stewart's fortunes were established. But he next appears in employment as a companion for a 'gentleman' and leaving for India, where he settled until returning with a legacy of £10,000, at which point he cannot have been older than 30. In Edinburgh he worked in a government tax department and was employed 'assiduously' for around 43 years, dying in his post in 1814.

Perhaps he was a clerk who worked his way up, or simply an astute Scot who invested wisely, never married and worked until he died. A

Daniel Stewart, whose name lives on in the Edinburgh school, was born and brought up at Strathtay, making his fortune variously in India and Edinburgh.

portrait of him by Sir Henry Raeburn hangs in the Merchants' Hall in Edinburgh, so he must have achieved the status of being a man of substance. But his heart was still in the highlands of Perthshire, as the terms of his last testament dictated. His will totalled £18,000, worth just under £1 million today. As a government clerk he would have earned around five times the annual wage of a farm labourer, so it can only have been assiduous saving from this salary, allied to his earnings from his time in India, which eventually realised the fortune he left at his death. But even this substantial amount was not to be used immediately for his cherished wish, to found schools in both Strathtay and Edinburgh. Firstly, his legacy was to provide for his invalid niece, and when that had been subtracted, the remainder was to be given to found the schools. Accordingly, the school of Strathtay was built in 1819 high up in the hills, close to his birthplace. It was a plain, three-storey house, with a plaque above the door. Initially, intake of pupils was limited to those with the surnames of Stewart and Macfarlane. The school bore the name, the Daniel Stewart

The first Daniel Stewart's school high up at Strathay, with the coat of arms above the doorway, no longer exists.

Free School. Perhaps his reasoning was that many of his relatives of those names still lived round the area, to whom he wished to offer education. But after all the Stewarts and Macfarlanes were admitted, and there were spare places for pupils, others were encouraged to enrol. Within another 20 years, the school was attracting pupils from much further afield. The school emerged as one of five in the vicinity, and the most successful. On 13 March 1857, there were 218 pupils enrolled, who were sitting an examination which was being assessed and marked by the local church minister. Winter attendance was much greater than in summer when the pupils were required for farm work. Winter timetables had to pack in many subjects, ranging from 'land measuring', to spelling, Bible studies and the history of Scotland, to 'practical gunnery'. From opening time at 10 a.m. to closure at 3.30 p.m., all this had to be accomplished by a headmaster and an assistant of maybe 18 years of age. The bad weather over the winter accounted for pupils arriving soaked and cold, or exhausted by battling through snowdrifts. Epidemics occasionally raged. But in the 75 or so years of the school's existence, the roll call of distinguished pupils ranged over many bearing both Stewart and Macfarlane surnames, and gradually – as an interesting aside – as many girls as boys achieved high marks.

By 1855, there was enough left in the kitty for the Daniel Stewart's School to be built in Edinburgh, and this school still flourishes in partnership with other educational establishments. It is now known as the Erskine Stewart's Melville Schools, and incorporates The Mary Erskine School, Stewart's Melville College and The Mary Erskine and Stewart's Melville Junior School. However, no school now exists on the original site overlooking Strathtay.

Earlier centres of learning had traditionally centred round ecclesiastical foundations. Dull is particularly connected with St Adamnan, also known as Eonan. Irish-born, he became the ninth abbot of Iona around AD 704 and had requested that, after his death, his body was to be carried east and, wheresoever the first 'withy' broke, there he was to be buried. This wish was carried out and the first 'withy' was said to have broken at Dull and there he was laid to rest. A community grew up around the chapel built at his grave site, and a monastery and college thrived there. Its endowments are said to have been transferred to St Andrews University when it was founded in 1413. Small monasteries were scattered throughout Perthshire, and apart from the four in Perth there were two other major Christian foundations, the abbey at Coupar Angus founded around the twelfth century and the earlier cathedral at Dunkeld founded around the ninth century. Both suffered catastrophic damage after the Reformation. The monks in Dunkeld, who had maintained the great cathedral and served the wider community, all disappeared and Perthshire was without a centre or training ground for priests of any denomination for three centuries.

But in 1838 there was a revival of the energy and vitality of the Scottish Episcopal Church. This marked a recovery from years of keeping a very low and discreet profile, as many Episcopalians had shown a public commitment to the Jacobite cause. Into this era emerged an ambitious new scheme, which was to build a school and theological college somewhere north of the Firth of Forth, but at a distance from any town. With re-invigorated zeal to nurture the faith by providing both a school for boys and a theological college for young men to enter the ministry, it was not to be established close to the temptations of a town and all the distractions this might offer. At the time there was nowhere for young men to prepare for ordination into the Episcopal Church, and the only method of studying theology was at a Scottish university, which were all, of course Presbyterian.

A small selection of the most eminent men of their generation undertook to found this college, and to search the substantial area north of the Firth of Forth for a likely spot to realise their dream. One supporter was Dean Edward Bannerman Ramsay, a high-ranking member of the Episcopal Church, as Dean of the Diocese of Edinburgh, and also with his own charge at St John's Church in Princes Street, Edinburgh. He enjoyed great popularity through his writings, which were filled with amusing anecdotes of his life in the church, and of the spirit and character of the Scots in general. He was not above poking fun at his fellow clergymen, and was a great man of the people. His observations of ordinary life are just as amusing today, and he was often referred to as being a 'colossus' astride the Episcopal Church in Scotland in the nineteenth century. His support of the project was greatly important. To establish a theological college in Scotland, as well as a new school to emulate the style of the great public (fee-paying) schools in England, certainly required someone of his eminence and charm.

He was assisted by two further staunch characters, William Ewart Gladstone, and James Hope. Gladstone was a son of Sir

John Gladstone, a businessman who had made a fortune from his plantations in the Caribbean, and who was an enthusiastic supporter of his son's interest in the project. William Ewart Gladstone was by then a Minister in Parliament, a serious character and High Tory who held deeply entrenched views on the church. He was interested in social deprivation and was beginning to take an interest in personally 'saving' prostitutes in London. The third member of the trio was James Hope, a grandson of the earl of Hopetoun and a friend of Gladstone's from their student days at Oxford. He described studying ecclesiastical law as enjoying his time in a flower garden, as opposed to dealing with parliamentary law which he likened to being in a cabbage patch. He married Charlotte Lockhart, a granddaughter of Sir Walter Scott, and subsequently changed his name to Hope-Scott.

These three forceful characters drove forward the project. Primarily they wished to establish a theological college for young men to study for ordination, and provide an Episcopalian school for the sons of the Scottish middle classes, who might not be able to afford to send their sons to the established fee-paying schools in England, or who might be unlikely to do so. Their new school would charge only half the amount of the fees.

They gathered together a substantial sum of money and set out in search of a suitable place to build the college. It is still possible to imagine the missionary zeal with which James Hope, Sir John Gladstone and his son and parliamentarian William, packed themselves into a post-chaise in the late summer of 1842, confident in the knowledge that cash was flowing in. Eventually, by 1846 or 1847, the sum totalled over £33,000, the equivalent of roughly £2.5 million today.

Sites in Perth itself were quickly rejected, as the proximity to the centre of a town with the temptations of pubs and other places of amusement went completely against one of their guiding principles. (It is interesting to note that the divinity students at St Andrews University wore black gowns, as opposed to the remainder of the students who wore red, because the divinity students were deemed to be beyond reproach. Therefore the red-gowned students would be instantly recognisable if embroiled in a disturbance. Such trust did not seem to apply to the potential theological students destined for the new theological college.)

Another site they viewed, near Rhynd, was deemed to be appealing as it offered an opportunity for plenty of good exercise on the river. Perhaps they were misjudging the strength of the Tay, confusing the type of boating there with punting at Oxford. From there they went to see Sir William Stewart's estate at Murthly, but this was also rejected on the grounds that the Stewarts were staunch Roman Catholics and, while they might be prepared to gift some ground, this might lead to confusion with their own religious beliefs. On they went to George Patton's estate of the Cairnies in Glenalmond.

Perhaps because of the long day, with the addition of a good luncheon at Cairnies, the decision was made. Sir John Gladstone apparently stuck his stick in the ground around where the present buildings of Glenalmond College now stand, and declared that he, for one, had made up his mind. The offer was tempting. Patton offered an initial plot of land free of charge, with the option of renting or purchasing more acres at a later date.

So the first Episcopal theological college and school, named Trinity College, finally opened its doors in 1847, with fourteen pupils and the Warden, or head of the college, Charles Wordsworth, a nephew of the poet William Wordsworth. Wordsworth had been the second master at Winchester when William Ewart Gladstone approached him, persuading him to come north. Gladstone later claimed that it was the best day's work he had done in his life. The salary was generous, at £700 per year with an intriguing bonus of £2 10s for each boy recruited after the first 80. The omens were bright.

Gavin White, an Honorary Canon of St Mary's Cathedral, Glasgow, wrote a history of the Episcopal Church and neatly summed up the ethos of the theological college combined with a school. Perhaps with tongue in cheek he divulged that 'The advantage of such a combination was that the fees for schoolboys would pay for the theological part of the enterprise, the headmaster doubling as theological tutor, and some gentility might rub off on the ordinands. So in 1847, Trinity College, Glenalmond, was founded in the middle of nowhere and midway between everywhere.'

Wordsworth, the Warden, was faced with this impossible task of dealing with two quite separate groups of pupils, and finally left the school in 1854. His successor seems to have treated the ordinands as schoolboys, even if he did not treat the schoolboys as ordinands. More seriously, the ordinands were 'of lower rank in life than the other members of the College', and this was obvious to the latter.

And the ordinands complained of 'under-education and lack of training'. It was little consolation that the graduates of the course were given the right to wear academic hoods; these garments were the subject of much debate and, at a time when Scottish universities did not award hoods, they gave Glenalmond a touch of Oxford or Cambridge respectability.

There exists a list of 21 clergy who studied under Wordsworth. But the system was failing. By 1880, not one divinity student remained. Any who wished to study moved to the more sensible location of Edinburgh where a theological college had been established in Coates Crescent, close to St Mary's Cathedral in Palmerston Place.

The closure of the theological department certainly angered some, who felt that they had been asked for cash on the wrong premise. The then Bishop of St Andrews was dismayed, declaring that he had helped to fund the chapel there, describing it accurately as a magnificent place of worship. He felt the grounds for abandoning the theological college were definitely questionable. But closed it was. The school flourishes, but as for a theological college in Perthshire, it was emphatically the end of the dream.

Almost exactly a century later, and in stark contrast to the founding of Trinity College Glenalmond, which was backed by a clutch of some of the most eminent men of the age, Rannoch School was a triumph of three teachers whose faith, grit and manual work virtually built the school. The idea of establishing Rannoch School, situated on the south side of Loch Rannoch, began in 1957 when Altyre School, an independent part of Gordonstoun, in Morayshire, was given notice to leave Altyre House.

Robert Chew, the Headmaster, asked various members of the staff to look at the possibility of finding another place for the school. However the governors of Gordonstoun decided to build a new Altyre House in the main school grounds, so the search for alternative accommodation was unnecessary. But the idea of another, smaller school had taken root, and three members of the Altyre staff continued their search with the idea of starting another school.

The founders, Dougal Greig, John Fleming, and Pat Whitworth, set out to find a suitable house. Quite a few places were looked at and dismissed until early in 1958 when Tom Duff, a builder friend of the Flemings, who lived in Strathtay, suggested they look at Dall House on the south shore of Loch Rannoch. This was up for sale from the

Forestry Commission who had bought it, and the surrounding land, from the heirs of Captain Vernon-Wentworth. Dall had been built in 1857 by George Duncan Robertson of Struan. The founders offered £1,500 for the house, walled garden, and a field beside the loch, about twenty-five acres in all.

Attempting to start a private, fee-paying boarding school from scratch was exceedingly ambitious. In addition to the worrying financial implications of establishing a new school, the requirement to find excellent teaching staff who would also be content to settle down in such a remote situation, and attract enough pupils was indeed a challenge. What was required initially, though, was the ability to deal with the day-to-day challenges of restoring a run down old house.

The creation of the school was carefully chronicled in a series of letters from Elizabeth Fleming, the wife of one of the founders, John Fleming, to her parents. She broke the news to her parents that they were setting up a new school in July 1958:

My dearest Mother and Father,

As I expect you have guessed we have become a bit unsettled with the prospect of the school closing in a few years time.

Two other masters, Dougal Greig and Pat Whitworth, and John have got together to form a company to start a new Independent Boarding School for boys, public school age. While retaining the Gordonstoun principles of character training through various activities, mountaineering and sailing.

We have found a very suitable house, Dall House on the southern shores of Loch Rannoch. It would house the entire staff and about 50 boys including library, assembly hall, classsrooms, etc. It is in quite good condition – needs painting and some minor repairs. Lovely situation close to the loch and the public road. It has a hard tennis court, boat house and boating rights on the loch (sailing, and swimming and rowing). Also a sizeable burn for fishing. Wonderful hills just behind (climbing, camping, skiing), curling rink, cricket pitch, fields for rugger, pony trekking (Dougal has been offered a present of up to 40 garrons!) – we'll have half a dozen or so!

One of the first purchases on behalf of the school was a pantechnicon from Thomas Love & Sons in Perth. One evening, there was an invitation from an old friend, Nancy Thorn, who owned the disused Ardeonaig Church, to accept, dismantle, and remove the 24-foot long pews for use at Rannoch. The pews were to be installed in a barrel-ceilinged room, above the south door, to form a chapel. Dougal, Pat and the Flemings went over to south Tayside in the pantechnicon, loaded the pews and after a pleasant meal set off home at 11 p.m. Pat was driving. The two Fleming children were asleep with Elizabeth in the front while Dougal and John made themselves comfortable in the Luton van. Half-way along the loch, Pat heard intermittent thumps overhead and stopped to investigate what was falling off. All was well, the noise being caused by Dougal and John attempting to open a beer bottle.

By early September 1958 great advances had been made, and for the first time, it was possible to have a hot bath with running water, and to accommodate household stores; 1200 empty bottles had to be cleared out. A great deal of time was spent in auction and MOD sales to furnish and equip the school.

The pantechnicon undertook sterling service backwards and forwards from Edinburgh to Rannoch, Moray to Rannoch, carrying absolutely everything from cutlery to electric generators, and flitting various married staff.

In August 1959 it was lent to Altyre School in Morayshire, who were producing their own show at the Festival Fringe in Edinburgh. To advertise this, a musical about Nessie, the van was beautifully painted with monsters on either side and the production name, 'Beastie Beware'. From then the van was known as Beastie and did all its future work for many years still in its fine paintwork, causing a great deal of curiosity when collecting such out of the way things as yet another generator from a scrapyard in Leith.

Nine months after her first letter to her parents, Elizabeth Fleming was applying herself to the finer details of clothing.

8 March 1959

Today I was in Inverness seeing to uniform. The samples of tweed [from Pringle's, Inverness and Ballantynes in the Borders] and jersey were not right so they have to try again. The shorts material is A1 [from Haggart's, Aberfeldy] – a kind of olive lovat green and very good stuff. So they are going to produce wool to tone with that

174

for the jersey and jacket. The uniform will not be cheap, but good and simple – not much of it.

15 March 1959

Our great new idea is that the burn near the sawmill has a dam, a lade etc. all more or less ready to be harnessed to produce electricity. Mr. O'Hagan, an Irish consultant Electrical Engineer, is most intrigued at the prospects and reckons that a volume Hydro plant [a Francis Turbine] there could produce 33 h.p. - or 25 Kw. That, if running all the time, would be enough to heat all the domestic hot water and boys' washroom water in Dall, and would produce in a year £1,300 worth of Electricity! - it should repay more than the capital outlay in the first year.

The future of the school was still sitting on a financial knife edge, with members of teaching staff turning their hands to any task which was required, either to paint walls, or show prospective parents around.

Elizabeth Fleming wrote with relief that

News of the plans for the School appeared in The Scotsman, Glasgow Herald, Dundee Courier and Daily Telegraph on Tuesday, 31st March, 1959. Two days later, over a hundred letters of enquiry were received by Dougal. Later, articles appeared in The Times Educational Supplement, the Scots Magazine, and the Scottish Field.

August 1959

The Clan Donachaidh Society agreed that any boy, who did not have his own tartan, could wear a Robertson kilt in recognition of the fact that Dall House had been built by a Chief of the clan.

On 24 September 1959 the first term started with eighty-two boys. As the first boy arrived wearing the new school uniform (bringing back memories of the many evenings spent discussing materials and colours) most people were caught secretly watching him getting out of Jimmy Duncan's taxi - he had in fact come all the way from Canada!

The school was finally open, just 14 months after Elizabeth Fleming had nervously written to her parents about their plans to begin this brand new venture.

While they might have predicted many incidents and successes, the challenges of running a school in one of the more remote areas of Scotland threw up many an unusual episode.

On the first free afternoon with no scheduled lessons, the village shop opened up for business, despite the shopowner's own half-day. When the shopkeeper later discovered goods missing, a boy not only confessed to shoplifting, but added that he had never found it so easy. He was despatched back to his parents the following day.

A few years later, in 1963, cycle rides to nearby Macgregors Cave became increasingly popular. This is a cleft in the rocks containing a stone seat and a clear view to the ruins of Dunalastair House, a mile or so away. It was to Dunalastair House that the main attention of the cycling expeditions was focused.

It transpired that boys had discovered the old cellars under the empty and ruined house, and had come across a supply of champagne well over a hundred years old. Some senior boys then set up a system of paying younger ones to fetch them supplies when required. Needless to say the stuff was quite undrinkable, which was why it was still in the cellar, and those who had partaken were extremely ill, thus ensuring the eventual discovery of the escapade.

Probably the biggest headache for the school was maintain the home-made electricity supply for lighting, boilers, etc.

The generators used to supply electricity to the school were many and varied – there was the original Pelton wheel, a small DC supply, which ran at night, a couple of big generators purchased in the Naval scrapyards in Rosyth, which were nicknamed 'Grandfather' and 'Great-grandfather', an even bigger Caterpillar generator with a donkey engine just to start it. For a time there was a Startomatic which would, with the aid of an old-fashioned street lamp clock, start on its own, a great boon for John, Pat and Diarmid who found that early start, cranking those engines, quite a strain – perhaps Diarmid had the right idea, it was known which was his duty week by the sight of his pyjama legs appearing under his trousers.

Once during classes it was noticed that the bulbs were getting brighter and brighter until they began exploding. The three electricians converged at the double on the generator sheds to find the Caterpillar's governor had stuck, the engine was literally running away - the only method of stopping it was to cut off the fuel supply. It was decided to install a larger oil tank for the boilers so an ex-tanker body was bought and buried under the south lawn. While being unloaded by a giant crane something was heard rattling around inside, and when the tank was tipped on its side out came an object which was instantly recognised as a 4-inch shell! The area was cleared, and John Fleming picked up the shell and drove to the old ice hole where it was left until the army came and dealt with it. On another occasion a phosphorus bomb which had lain in the burn since the war was found in the forest and brought to Pat Whitworth who hastily immersed it in a bucket of water. The next day he dropped it in the middle of the loch.

Needless to say, various problems arose by having ponies at the Barracks so far from the school; once a pony was seen literally shaking a sheep which subsequently died, to the fury of the local farmer!

The Tuck Shop started in a cubbyhole in the main building and was run by Jane and Elizabeth with a team of boys. It later moved to a hut built by the Building Service close to the Potteries. There must have been huge sales because the profits were sufficient to tarmacadam the tennis court, purchase a projector and cinema screen, and other items.

When the lorry carrying the hot tarmac stuck in deep mud beyond the tennis court, the men said there was nothing they could do except dump it where it was. Boys turned to with shovels and wheelbarrows and had it all laid before it hardened.

Sheer physical effort, iron willpower, inspiration, and perhaps isolation contributed to the Rannoch School's success. But times were changing, and perhaps it was the isolation which contributed to attracting fewer pupils. Parents were more reluctant to send their children too far from home. For 40 years the school had flourished until falling rolls led to its closure in 2002.

Of the many schools which existed in Perthshire over the twentieth century, none was as questionable in its conception as the Aldour School, situated at the southern entrance to Pitlochry, where a small industrial centre now stands. Aldour was an 'experimental school' founded for the children who came from itinerant families, commonly referred to as tinkers, travellers or gypsies. This small building, which appears in a grainy photograph to be made from corrugated iron, was to house the children for their schooling. The school itself opened its doors in 1938, at a cost of £800, a considerable sum to raise.

The idea that this was to be an 'experimental school' sits uneasily today. Travellers, or tinkers, were not universally regarded as harmless. Serious curtailing of their travelling way of life had begun towards the end of the 1800s.

A contemporary account from a parish magazine in the Pitlochry area explained the reasoning behind the 'special' school.

> The wandering gypsy folk are a strange and picturesque survival from the early nomadic days of civilization. One would be sorry to see these dweller in tents and lovers of the open road pass from our countryside. But the training of their children presents a problem that is not easily solved. It has been found that as a rule they make better progress when taught by themselves and not alongside of children from a different environment. So this school has been provided for tinkers' children only. It is by nature of an experiment, and its progress will be followed with keen interest.

The founding of the school in 1938 with the clear intent of keeping gypsy children away from local children was typical of the thinking at the time. These incoming and itinerant children were regarded with suspicion by many in the communities within which they travelled. Who knows now quite what was behind the 'experiment'? With the onset of war, though, the school was doomed to last a short time, and closed its doors in 1941.

But while the isolation of schools such as Rannoch militated against their survival, the age of enjoying Perthshire, for just that reason had arrived. Tourism was on the cusp of developing into one of Perthshire's major industries.

CHAPTER 8
LEISURE AND PLEASURE

The military roads dug out of the land by Field Marshal George Wade between 1728 and 1730 were utilitarian and intended only for the efficient transportation of soldiers, rather than the convenience of pedestrians. With the ending of the Jacobite uprisings after 1745, the arrival of peaceful times and the travels of Thomas Pennant in the 1770s, Scottish tourism had a hesitant birth.

That Thomas Pennant visited Scotland was fortuitous. At the time the reputation of Scotland as a wild land fraught with danger still lingered on. He studied at Oxford, although he left before completing his degree. He came from a privileged background of landed gentry in Wales and while his specialist knowledge was natural history, he was also well read in topography and antiquities.

It was while at Oxford he discovered his passion was travel. He developed into an expert travel writer, being curious and interested in every aspect of the country through which he passed. He had a natural aptitude for making friends and a journalist's eye for spotting subjects which he judged to be of interest to his readers.

In visiting Scotland when he did, he paved the way for other travellers, describing the astonishing scenery and a country just waiting to be discovered. Being wealthy, he was also able to travel and write unfettered by the requirement to generate an income, and he was further in a position to employ illustrators, which added greatly to the success of his books.

In contrast to the Grand Tour, which was undertaken by sons of the landed gentry to visit to the cultural wonders of Italy, France and Greece, Pennant described a more modest route within Scotland, engagingly known as the Petit Tour, which is still popular today. A section of the route followed from Tyndrum, Crianlarich, Killin and Kenmore via Dunkeld to Perth, elevating Dunkeld into the main conduit through which most tourists had to travel. Followers of St

The Bailie Nicol Jarvie Inn at Aberfoyle, named after a character in Sir Walter Scott's novel about Rob Roy's adventures in the area. A favorite stopping-off place much used by such magnificent stage coaches.

Columba had trodden a similar route as they fanned out to spread the Christian word more than a thousand years before Pennant.

For the vast majority of those travelling in the late eighteenth and early nineteenth century, travelling was done mainly on foot. A few merchants and professional men would have owned and ridden on their horses, and some would have used their farm horses or oxen to pull farm carts. Coaches would only have been used by the very wealthy. Many of the routes followed were passable only on foot or horseback, and have been bypassed or sidelined as easier methods of travel have evolved.

Queen Victoria travelled over from Balmoral on Deeside on horseback to visit the dukes of Atholl at Blair Castle, as well as Dunkeld, and even slept the night in the Atholl Hotel in Dunkeld on 11 September 1844. Her travels certainly propelled the Blair Atholl area of Perthshire towards becoming a desired tourist destination.

But an appreciation of the area's beauty was not confined only to those travelling up from the south, nor was walking, as a means of getting from one place to another, only for those who could not afford another method of travel, such as riding within the shelter of a stagecoach.

A century on from Queen Victoria's visit, walking for pleasure was growing in popularity – although the irony cannot be lost on those whose only method of getting across the country was trudging on foot, that walking became a pastime for those wealthy enough to afford other means of transport.

One such devotee of long-distance walking was the intrepid Sir James Ramsay, father of Katherine, the 'Red' Duchess of Atholl. Katherine was born in 1874 at the family home at Banff, a house three miles northwest of Alyth. Her mother died when she was young, and her father brought up his children alone. He was a fearless mountaineer, a fitness enthusiast and a member of the Alpine Club. In response to a query by King George V as to just how he kept so fit though over 90 years old, he explained briskly that it was 'temperate living, and plenty of work both inside and out of doors'.

He celebrated his 80th birthday in 1912 by a walking-trip over the hills by way of Lochnagar, accompanied by two of his daughters. The following extract is taken from Sheila J. Heatherington's *Katherine Atholl 1874–1960: Against the Tide* (AUP, 1989):

They carried no map, but as on other occasions many years before, Sir James expected to be given directions at a cottage known as Bachnagairn. This proved to be an empty ruin, so they simply climbed from the south west along a ridge until they could see the top of the mountain beyond. By the time they reached the summit daylight was already fading and they took a short cut off the track, following the line of a stream which they knew must lead to the River Dee and Braemar. They reached the road as darkness fell, but had several further hours of walking towards Braemar – the sisters holding hands and singing hymns – until, at midnight they arrived at their destination, although there was some difficulty waking the staff. They had walked 25 miles, climbed over some 5,000 feet and crossed some very rough moorland. After a day's rest at Braemar they set out again, to walk down to Glen Tilt – a wild mountain path – to visit Katherine (she had married John, Duke of Atholl in

Resting at Bridge of Cally, a much used route for hundreds of years.

1899) at Blair Castle, a further distance of 25 miles and at least 1,000 feet of climbing; no mean feat.

Sir James Ramsay died in 1925, aged 92.

Long-distance walking of this type gave way to other ideas about leisure and tourism. Towns such as Pitlochry, Crieff and Callander, and many other smaller places, such as St Fillans, Birnam and Strathtay, experienced a building boom from the middle to the end of the nineteenth century when the railway arrived. To accommodate tourists, houses could be let, lucratively, for part of the year, while the owners down-sized to a small cottage at the foot of the garden.

Railway companies found other methods to cater for the tourist trade besides transporting holiday-makers to their destination. In 1933 the enterprising company of London and North Eastern Railway simply 'parked' their sleeping-coaches at the side of a branch line at Strathyre and proceeded to let them as small-scale holiday cottages. This presented an affordable holiday for those who might never

Bus manoevering the notorious double bends of the A93, Devils Elbow Road from Glenshee to Braemar. By the 20th century, the tourist industry had discovered Perthshire and exploration by bus was a popular method of viewing the countryside.

before have been able to go away, or who might have been restricted to a couple of nights in a guest house within a short distance of one of the big cities.

A week's rental was around £3, and each coach could accommodate around six people tucked into either two or four cabins, with a dining room in the middle, and a kitchen at one end. As the average yearly wage for a labourer or craftsman was between £125 and £165, this made a holiday possible. These coaches were parked all over the country at known beauty spots, and continued to be popular until well into the 1960s, when more sophisticated holidays in better quality self-catering cabins or cottages were sought, and the closure of so many smaller routes by Beeching put an end to railway lines in these more remote and picturesque areas.

Travelling on water through Perthshire had also been strictly a method of getting from one destination to another. Ferries were evident at every possible safe crossing place over the great rivers and lochs, while on the latter would be seen large rowing craft and steamers used to transport passengers and goods. Coal was a classic cargo, and was carried from one end of Loch Tay to be landed on another shore close to habitations. But as the country became more attractive for leisure activities, more pleasure craft began to appear, until it seemed that every loch in Perthshire had its quota.

For many of their owners it was a purely extravagant gesture, rather than a commercial exercise. Some were launched by enterprising local businessmen who viewed the arriving visitors as a financial opportunity, and came up with ideas for their entertainment. Sightseeing on board a small steamer or paddle boat offered one possibility. Whereas many of these entrepreneurs could only operate during the summer months, for a local laird with a deep purse this was not a consideration. One laird built a boat purely for his own use.

A first-hand account of such a boat-building enterprise was written by Duncan McDonald who spent over fifty years as a blacksmith in Kinloch Rannoch. Born in 1837, he first lived and worked in Blair Atholl, and moved to Kinloch Rannoch in 1884 where he kept a watchful eye on the local goings-on, while working away steadily at his smiddy. His writings display a pithy humour, are surprisingly romantic, and have a wide-ranging, wholly independent approach to observing those around him, no matter which social class they belonged to.

Later he became a Justice of the Peace in the area, and his shrewd observations, about the battles between the local lairds, for example, must have provided him with light relief from his hammering. Duncan made it his business to get on well with the local lairds, but he had a mixed relationship with his nearest neighbour and namesake, General Macdonald. On the one hand, he was grateful for the generosity shown by the General in converting and improving his smiddy, while on the other, he was vexed about the his intransigence when it came to the toll he was charged on the road. The General refused to budge over his ownership of the road to Trinafour. It was his road, and he exacted tolls and refused to listen to demands for it to be made up into a public road. For Duncan McDonald, the tolls were a bitter pill as this was the only way to go to the railway station at Struan to collect the supplies of iron and coal for his smiddy. But despite this his business flourished, and he once described how he had a pile of old horseshoes over 28 feet high, so busy was his blacksmith shop

Straloch, on the road from Kirkmichael over to Blairgowrie, is still recognizable, and the houses predating these ones would have seen many a droving season.

at the height of the expansion of the area and in the final heyday of horse-drawn traffic in the dying days of the nineteenth century.

As Duncan's written story unfolds, it appears he had developed a soft spot for his local laird, and never more so than when his steamship *Gitana* sank. The blacksmith's grandson, Duncan McDonald Sinclair, recorded many of his stories, such as the sad, but epic tale of the steamship and the ensuing and long-running confrontation between Duncan and General Macdonald. Duncan described the event;

I felt really sorry for the General, the day the *Gitana* sank.

It wasn't just the expense, though it must have cost him a fortune, but it had been such a tremendous struggle for him to put her on the Loch at all. Building Dalchosnie Lodge and Dunalastair House and the new hotel and even at the Episcopal Church were great things for the village, and no doubt cost a lot of money, but they were improvements that any landlord could make, and indeed many a laird has done more. But he had the steam boat designed and built in three sections, each one to be brought by road from Glasgow, and that meant a hundred miles of slow heavy haulage, by means of big slow horses. How it ever reached here, I can't imagine. Then the three parts were put together, in the yard behind the hotel, and at last put in the water, complete with engine and coal and all the necessities, even wee lamps on the cabin walls, as neat as you like; it was a great achievement, right enough.

Of course, a man doesn't get to be a general without facing problems and sorting them out. Even planning and making his private road, across the moor to Trinafour – some undertaking that was, too. And I think putting a steamer on Loch Rannoch became a great ploy for the General – like a laddie with a new toy really. But he reckoned without one thing, or maybe two: the stupidity of the Rannoch Lairds, and the ferocity of the Rannoch weather.

Yes, I've always thought that Sir Robert Menzies was a stupid man, though he had been to Oxford or wherever. It riled me every year when I had to write to the Menzies Estate office or Castle Menzies for permission to go across to Glengoulandie and cut a puckle [small amount] bracken, for the tattie [potatoes] pit and for bedding my cattle here. My goodness, Sir Robert should have been paying men like to me to keep cutting the bracken back, but he was too stupid to see it. Thirty years behind the times, and more. They just weren't ready for a steamboat out on the Loch, and went to law to try to stop it – what foolishness, just more money in the lawyer's pockets. They said the *Gitana* would spoil the fishing, but the Edinburgh Sheriffs weren't as daft as to believe that. The Menzies witnesses were then ready to swear all manner of things, but the judges said that on any loch in the Highlands, you could find old men who would swear the sport was better 40 years ago that it is now!

Then, having lost that battle, Sir Robert and his friends were determined that the steamer shouldn't be moored in any of the sheltered corners near their property, so the General just had to leave [her] where he could, and of course the storm came, the waves broke her fancy wee windows, and down she went. What a shame. But by God's mercy there was no one aboard at the time. The General had built a wee shack, beside Ellen Dewar's cottage, and he had a rope from the ship and the bell on it so he would wake if

Steamer moored close to the pier at Kenmore, a faster method of transport than the roads.

the wind got up. Much good that did, with the bonnie *Gitana* about a hundred feet down, in no time at all.

Other steamships cruised on other lochs with less dramatic results. The final trip on a steamer called *Queen of the Lake* on Loch Tay was in 1939. The steamer had offered a popular and well-organised outing from such places as Ballinluig. Here the garage operated a charabanc (a type of bus, sometimes horse-drawn) early in the nineteenth century, and later a bus or taxi service to Kenmore, from where passengers boarded the steamer down to Killin to partake of tea, followed by the return journey to Kenmore and the bus home.

Loch Earn, one more of the great lochs in Perthshire, also offered unique water sports.

Motorized water sports began on Loch Earn during the summer of 1955 with the discovery of an elderly Chris Craft which had been put up on blocks in 1939. It had acted as a rescue boat for John Cobb during his speed trials on Loch Ness. It was bought by Ewen Cameron, proprietor of the Lochearnhead Hotel at the western end of the loch, and brought to Loch Earn. Ewen's wife Ann Cameron bravely volunteered to be towed behind on a 'ski' gleaned from the bonnet of a Morris Minor 1000. But when one of the Camerons returned from a summer holiday with a pair of water skis and the knowledge of how to do it, water skiing on Loch Earn was born.

By the spring of 1956 Ewen Cameron had formed a club with members paying a debenture of £50.00 (this would be around £1000 today) and soon had enough members to enable them to buy two Albatrosses and go into business.

Wetsuits were unknown, so woolly sweaters were often worn, and life jackets were bought from ships being broken up at Rosyth, both heavy and cumbersome.

In August of that year a privately owned modern Chris Craft arrived and it was a privilege to be offered a tow behind this monster. Everything was fun, and the members invented and learnt all sorts including parachutes, loaned by some of the members from Leuchars, being towed behind boats, kites to which one could be attached, discs on which to rotate, boards on which one would sit and a second would stand, jumping, slalom and other tricks.

By the end of that first summer, friends from the south had discovered the club and became interested in holding competitions on Loch Earn as this was the only stretch of water without restrictions at that time.

The Club were talked into organising the Scottish Native Championship in 1957 to be followed by the British Water Ski Championship over the next two years.

In 1963, the Northern European Championships was held at Lochearnhead under the auspices of the World Water Ski Association. Competitors from eleven countries took part in this event which was sponsored by the *Daily Telegraph*, Bells Whisky and many other local firms. Over 10,000 people came to spectate and every hotel, B&B and guest house from Callander to Comrie and Killin were occupied by officials and competitors. TV cameras were present and the event was recorded. All the fields at the Lochearnhead end became a tented village with sponsors and trade tents selling their wares.

Fancy Dress BBQs – rare in those days – ceilidhs in Lochearnhead and Grand Balls in London brought in funds to strengthen the Club. Many times World Champion, Mike Hazlewood, first learnt to ski on Loch Earn as did one time ladies' World Champion, Phillipa Roberts.

The trajectory of the club was going ever upwards into major competitions.

In 1969 Italy was unable to take on the finals of the European Championships and the Lochearnhead Water Ski Club was asked to host the event. Boating on Loch Earn in those early days was controlled by a 'dictatorship' headed by an efficient retired banker from St Fillans. He patrolled the loch at weekends and any boat launching for a days 'jolly' was charged 10/-. If the boat launched did not get a ticket first – these were sold in the village shops – no one would permit them to land until such time as they paid up!

Water skiing was given the royal seal of approval when Prince Philip heard what was happening and arrived by helicopter to see for himself what was going on.

Top competition came to an end when skiing became more money orientated and all skiers wanted to ski in waters of the same conditions as the previous competitors and this just could not be guaranteed on Loch Earn. So not only did the international championships come to an end on Loch Earn, so too came the demise of the nostalgic days of woolly sweaters and improvising skis made from car bonnets. Skiing is still very much part of life on Loch Earn but the days of leading the country in water skiing had gone.

Also vanished is the Lochearnhead Hotel which was such a hub, not only for water skiing but because of the sheer exuberance of its owners and the many famous guests who visited.

The inn at Lochearnhead was built between 1746 and 1751. Local legend has it that the illustrious Field Marshal Wade was reputed to have remarked that the existing inn provided accommodation not fit to put an animal inside. The old inn had already been standing for over a century when, in 1870, the Callander to Oban railway was built through Glen Ogle, and was later extended along the line to St Fillans and Crieff.

Queen Victoria described the Glen Ogle Pass as 'the Khyber

The Lady of the Lake plied her trade up and down Loch Tay, taking day trippers sailing up and down the 15 miles of loch from Kenmore to Killin.

Pass of the North'. It was the best advertising slogan from the most influential person in the United Kingdom, and produced a rapid building of a plethora of hotels.

One of the several large hotels which rose to the challenge of this boom was the Lochearnhead Hotel owned by the Cameron family who became famous in the area for several generations. The old inn had been rebuilt in about the 1890s, at the time that the railway line had been extended as far as on Loch Earn. It must have been just after this time that, during the building of the railway line, some of the metal rails found their way into the roof space of the hotel and were inserted in place of rafters. Between these metal struts the space was filled up with clinker which would have been the remains from coal fires, and a common enough material used for insulation and sound-deadening.

The Camerons moved from Fort William to Lochearnhead and bought the hotel in the early part of the twentieth century. It became a flourishing family hotel. More accommodation was added, as well as, in 1934, a new front with a long glazed area. In the 1950s when the next generation took over, Ewen and Ann Cameron, the hotel

Water skiing became a very popular sport on Loch Earn for many years. Mrs Anne Cameron, wife of the Lochearnhead Hotel Proprietor Ewen Cameron first water skied by using the bonnet of a Morris Minor car.

entered a new stage. Their energy appeared awe-inspiring. Not only was Ewen a huge character with a massive physical presence, he had been born to be a hotelier. At 6 feet 5 inches tall he was also one of the greatest 'heavies' on the Highland Games circuit.

By the time he reinstated the local Lochearnhead Highland Games, his established success as a notable heavyweight athlete meant that he had claimed over a hundred first prizes over a season when he was competing. Ewen's 22-stone weight was deceptive, owing to his height, and he had a 53-inch chest, 16-inch biceps and 36-inch thighs. On one occasion Ewen packed up his caber and went off on his own to Denmark to appear before 30,000 spectators proving, as always, a wonderful ambassador for Scotland.

But his success on the games circuit did not detract from his ambitions for the hotel. In 1957 he and Ann added a big ballroom, with reputedly the best sprung dance floor after that at Gleneagles. They added private bathrooms adjacent to all the bedrooms over a period of 20 years, manoeuvring the facilities into spaces sandwiched between the ancient core of the building and later additions. Quite often they had no idea of what they were going to find at the back of walls pierced to insert plumbing. Eventually the hotel could sleep between 80 and 90 people, but in high days and holidays, such as Hogmanay, many more were squeezed in. The hotel rose in prominence and earned a reputation as one of the finest hotels in Scotland. When Prime Minister Margaret Thatcher was visiting Glasgow in the 1980s, on a visit when the heckling was particularly bruising for her, her procession of cars, which was being trailed by the press up the main A9, succeeded in losing all followers at the Kier roundabout north of Stirling, and made for the Lochearnhead Hotel. It was an ideal spot to get away from it all. She had been expected to go to Gleneagles, and the trailing press cars were left to pursue a false trail

The Camerons had told Mrs Thatcher's entourage that a wedding was taking place within the hotel that day between a girl who was very Tory, and her husband-to-be who was a Liberal. They duly pulled up in front of the hotel, where the wedding was in full swing, and greeted the guests. She was to be one of the last of the famous guests.

During the night of 5 November 1982, Guy Fawkes Night, just after the hotel had been closed down at the end of the season, a disastrous fire ripped through the entire building.

Curlers enjoying the 'roaring game' outside on Polney Loch, by Dunkeld.

Adjacent to the main road between Aberfeldy and Grandtully is an overgrown curling pond, with this enchanting wooden pavilion, long disused. Most small towns, villages and even hamlets possessed their own outdoor rink, usually well screened from the south, to ensure the pond remained frozen for as long as possible. None appear to be used today.

To this day the origins of the fire remain a mystery, despite many forensic experts sifting through the rubble. The Camerons had left to stay in Elie, but before they left, had turned off all the electricity within the hotel and there was not a soul inside.

By the time the fire was noticed, it proved impossible to contain. All that had survived, when the Camerons returned the next day, were some of the outer walls and the new extension which had been added as a public bar a few years before. It was never rebuilt. Today some very ordinary residential houses sit on top of what had enjoyed a century of hotel success.

Little remains of the other popular leisure activity that took off in the 1920s – cinema-going. Only one of the 12 cinema buildings in Perthshire has survived in its intended purpose as a 'picture house', as a place of escape for families to come and see a world which they were unlikely to experience unless on celluloid. The only original cinema still in use is the Playhouse in Perth.

Cinemas in Scotland are increasingly rare now, and the numbers in Perthshire echo this trend. Although some of the wonderful Art Deco buildings have vanished, and others are derelict, there is an encouraging and growing band of local folk all over the country who are now realising just what a loss this might be, and who wish to restore them.

The result is that some of these 1930s buildings, having lived through many uses and incarnations, are now being saved and re-opened, for example to fulfil a role as part-cinema, part-café and part-community meeting place. One, interestingly, is now a church. Most cinemas in Perthshire are typical of the period in which they were built, the 1920s or 1930s. The rise of television in the 1960s and 70s saw the role and use of the cinema diminish.

The history of showing films in Scotland commenced around 1896, with showings in Edinburgh, Glasgow and Aberdeen that year. A few years later, some High Street shop owners woke up to the new trend and rapidly converted their premises to accommodate the new fashion. To encourage larger audiences, films were also shown in large fairground tents, replete with the elaborate awnings typical of their heritage as travelling circuses or fairground entertainment. However, the equipment to show films was highly flammable, and it was the legislation which sought to protect the public which opened

The picture house in Coupar Angus was originally a church, and has now reverted to the purpose for which it was built.

the way for purpose-built cinemas. The Cinematograph Act of 1910 decreed that the projection rooms should be separate from the audience, for their own safety.

Specialist architects sprang up to offer their services. While the old music halls or theatres offered customers elaborate plaster ceilings and walls, this decoration was found to interfere with the sound quality, and so a whole new approach was required. Acoustic specialists came onto the scene, and the requirements of the new buildings offered architects a chance to indulge in the latest architectural style. As these extraordinary new stucco-clad buildings appeared, totally unlike most of the style of the average Perthshire High Street, they reflected all the modern, fairy-tale life that Hollywood had to offer.

Cinema attendance grew rapidly, because it was one of the few, inexpensive ways that families could have an outing together, or that children could be sent off to, or to get out of a crowded house on a Saturday morning. It also brought the newsreels to ordinary folk.

Cinemas were warm and offered an escape from the often extremely harsh life of the era. The 1930s in Perthshire were affected by the economic depression, much like the rest of the country, and for a few hours cinema-goers would be able to leave this behind. Just how popular the cinemas were is reflected the changeover of films, often every three days, and demonstrates why small towns in Perthshire not only attracted audiences of a hundred or so, with a building to accommodate them all, but occasionally even had two cinemas in the same town.

Two towns in Perthshire supported two cinemas, while Crieff appeared to offer three venues for the local residents. Auchterarder had the Regal in the High Street, which now is condemned and, at the time of writing, is about to be demolished. The glass-filled front on the High Street was elaborately decorated inside, with a pressed tin roof, a tea area, and an impressively gracious staircase. It eventually became an antiques shop.

The second cinema in Auchterarder was called the Good Templar Hall, in Abbey Road, and originally showed silent films. Eventually it became a cash-and-carry and now is a children's nursery.

The Picture House in Reform Street, Blairgowrie, now lies sadly derelict. The front is plain 1930s stucco, with the gable end wall constructed into a curved brick wall. The second cinema, the Regal, at Bridgend appears just as ambitious a building, opened on 18 July 1938, later reincarnated as a bingo hall from April 1970 and then demolished in the early 1990s to be replaced by residential apartments. The drawing which graced the brochure for the official opening clearly demonstrates just what a sophisticated image the owners wished to convey.

One of Crieff's original cinemas still stands, but few would recognise the building's original purpose. Erected in 1924, with 650 seats for the Strathearn Cinema Company, it was built by a remarkable entrepreneur Peter Crerar, who ran a coach-building business and a steamer on Loch Earn which he had hauled by steam tractor from Perth. The story goes that the cinema was originally to be a garage, but when he became convinced that cinemas were the

The forlorn building which was once one of the cinemas in Blairgowrie hides a past when going to the cinema was a popular and weekly outing for many of the local residents.

thing of the future, he rushed up and stopped the men on the job, telling him they were now to build his new cinema.

Another of Crieff's cinemas, the Porteous Hall, on Strathearn Terrace, and variously named the Regal, Ritz or Rex, was sold to Morrison's Academy to be their refectory, but the saddest loss was an elegant stone building in Commissioner Street, which, when it closed as a cinema, became the home for Meadow Motors and was eventually demolished.

In Station Road, Kinross, a private company was formed to acquire land for the purpose of erecting a cinema, and on 26 March 1938 the County Cinema opened its doors for 600 people, although this number of seats was rapidly reduced when the canny owners realised they then became liable for Entertainment Tax. It was still listed as a cinema in 1980, but then became a bingo hall before being demolished.

Perhaps the most curious of all is the Picture Playhouse in Queen Street, Coupar Angus, which was originally a church, with a frontage being added in the 1930s. This impressive frontage still remains, and after its demise as a cinema it reverted to being used as a church for a while.

In Pitlochry, a cinema called the Regal, in West Moulin Street, seated around 400, but was the forerunner of a much more ambitious form of visual entertainment. Nowhere in Perthshire could boast of a purpose-built theatre outside Perth, but this was about to change as a result of the ambitious changes which had taken place in the areas adjacent to the small town.

When the project of building hydroelectric dams in Perthshire was first aired, residents were fearful that the plan to build one of the dams at Pitlochry would be a death knell for tourism, which sustained both Pitlochry and the surrounding area.

Following the war, in the early 1950s, tourism had maintained its highly successful status. Historically this success had benefited greatly from the arrival of the railway line from Perth in 1863, a line which was later extended to Aviemore. Bringing the train to Pitlochry had certainly not been without opposition. Objections flowed from the pens of art critic John Ruskin and pre-Raphaelite painter Sir John Everett Millais, both of whom carried out a heated written defence of the area within the letters page of *The Times*.

Inevitably, the railway did arrive, with one of the first passengers being no less illustrious than Queen Victoria, who was on a visit to the sixth duke of Atholl before his imminent death. Pitlochry as a holiday destination was born. Hotels sprang up, and visitors flocked to the area. But by the middle of the twentieth century, entertainment was limited to a cinema and various amusements in local halls. A man already immersed in the thespian world, John Stewart, arrived with a grand idea, 'When staying in Pitlochry during the early part of the war, I chanced to see a stately house with a fairly large garden, quite close to the town. I at once realised that here my dream theatre might well be established in this fashionable resort right in the heart of Scotland'.

The theatre was the life-long passion of John Stewart. In the 1940s he was the director of a commercial college in Glasgow, Skerry's, which must have given him the background in management required for running an organisation. But he had already dipped his toes in the world of theatre. He had been a founder of the amateur 'Curtain Theatre' which had encouraged such talents as Duncan Macrae, whose fame as an actor ranged from appearing in *Whisky Galore* to *Tunes of Glory* and, most memorably as the captain of the Clyde puffer in *Para Handy*. Also a member of the 'Curtain Theatre' was playwright Robert McLellan, whose plays written in the Scots dialect also became famous.

Stewart pursued this interest in the theatre by then establishing the Park Theatre Club in Glasgow's West End in 1941. Dubbed 'Glasgow's First Little Theatre', it grew in stature to the point of having a fully professional cast by the time it closed in 1949, but with no prospect of a larger theatre being built in Glasgow, Stewart reluctantly 'shut the doors'. Stewart declared, somewhat obliquely in his final curtain speech, that 'Glasgow's loss will be Scotland's gain'.

It was again to Pitlochry that he looked. Local legend relates that he had hidden a slip of paper somewhere in the area during the war, on which was written: 'When peace is declared I shall return to this spot to give thanks to God and to establish my Festival'. Apparently, Stewart recovered that same slip of paper on VE Day, and vowed again to fulfil his promise. With such a rich seam of experience behind him, John Stewart's idea of founding a theatre in Pitlochry should have been welcomed with open arms by all its residents and all its officials.

But what was to become a familiar tale of delays and disappointments commenced. A site at Knockendarroch House beckoned. But 1949 was still a period of rationing of all building materials. Licences were needed from the Ministry of Works, who would issue them for essential building purposes only. So it was that the fledgling theatre company had also to apply. Despite a vigorous press campaign justifying their requirements on the grounds that tourism would benefit, that much-needed American tourist dollars would be earned, that the theatre would be an asset to Scotland, and that, anyway, the money to be spent would come from John Stewart's own funds, the request was refused.

Stewart then had a trump card up his sleeve. Inspired by the precedent of a tent theatre in Regent's Park in London, and

Birmingham's Arena Theatre, he proposed copying their enterprising streak and applied to erect a tent. Both the theatre tents in London and Birmingham had been supplied by the same company in Walsall. Stewart consulted them, agreed on a design and purchased his tent. Then a link with the Pitlochry dam emerged in an unlikely form.

Tom Johnston, who, as Secretary of State for Scotland had pushed through the hydroelectric schemes all over Scotland, and so had been in the forefront of the bitter battle to secure the dams near Pitlochry, also happened to be chairman of the Scottish Tourist Board. Existing opposition to the tent theatre in Pitlochry from the Ministry of Works evaporated and permission was given for a modest amount of steel and timber, so that the tented theatre could be completed. Finally, on 19 May 1951, Pitlochry Festival Theatre opened with the British première of Maxwell Anderson's *Mary of Scotland*, with Joss Ackland as Darnley. In his opening address Johnston declared, 'This theatre is a monument to one man's courage, one man's persistence, and one man's great faith'. That statement might be regarded, in the light of a six-year battle, as an understatement. But Johnston was a man who had also battled for many years for his own dream of the hydroelectric dams. If anyone was qualified to recognise a struggle, it was himself. But all this optimism proved to be short-lived. 1952 brought unexpected trouble. A storm broke in August that year which ripped the tent canvas right to the top of one of the king poles, thus compounding the theatre's financial plight. The loss for the first season had been £12,000 and £5,000 for the second, causing Stewart's accountant to warn him of possible bankruptcy if things continued on their present course. After due consideration, solace and advice were sought from an old friend, James Shaw Grant, editor of the *Stornoway Gazette* and later to be Chairman of the Board of Governors of Pitlochry Theatre, Stewart decided to continue, taking Grant's advice. He handed over his house, grounds, workshops and what was left of the tent theatre as a gift to the Pitlochry Festival Society. In return he was appointed festival director, with the right to live in what had been his own home. Kenneth Ireland, with whom Stewart had visited Pitlochry in 1944, was appointed general manager and company secretary of the Festival Theatre Society.

Support from the Arts Council to the tune of £250 for each of two plays – *The Rivals* and *The Importance of Being Earnest* – helped the theatre to end the 1953 season with a surplus of £1,000 and a new

The first theatre in the hills was was within a marquee at Pitlochry, and this subsequently became well known as the Pitlochry Festival Theatre.

feeling of confidence. It was during the early part of that year that work began on a new, much modified and improved theatre – the result of a special building appeal.

The original theatre tent was actually two tents, the inner one holding the 500-seat auditorium, while the outer was used for the foyer and restaurant. While the productions became successful and the theatre scraped by financially, ironically it was the very structure which aided its popularity and fame. There was something romantically appealing about attending a theatre in the hills, and while the staff understandably longed for a more functional venue, the audience was enchanted.

But the theatre outgrew both its original double tent, and the steel outer case. In order to continue, and construct a larger, purpose-built structure, another lengthy battle began. The determination of a few to raise the money required, for such a project, and to find a site, lasted many years. Thirty years after that first performance in a tent, the new Pitlochry Festival Theatre opened its doors in 1981. Inside there are pictures of the original tent, but as for the tented theatre itself, in the hills, not a trace remains.

Perhaps John Stewart, who had died suddenly in 1957, was allowing himself a wry grin at the chosen production, the title of which spoke volumes of the lengthy struggle to establish the theatre. The production was *Storm in a Teacup*. Now the theatre not only entertains many from a much-used stage, but also entertains new generations of theatre-goers who can dine overlooking the ever-moving force of the River Tay below.

Often locals and visitors alike appear to spend much time simply gazing at the mesmerizing waters of the great river of Perthshire, or the cascading rush of waterfalls from the steeply rising hills. So it seems completely appropriate that rushing water is the magnificent focus of Perthshire today.

The great River Tay has been, and remains to this day the spine of Perthshire. Powerful and occasionally unpredictable, it has caught many an inhabitant on its shores unawares, flooding many low-lying areas, and, even within living memory, transforming Perth itself into a Venice of Scotland

The rivers of the Tay, Earn, Almond and many others have supplied generations with the ability to earn a living from harnessing water power for mills, enabling weaving and milling. Fishing for salmon has fed the inhabitants for thousands of years, and allowed communications. The many rivers and burns which feed into the rivers of considerable length have also supplied the water for whisky distilling, the irrigation for sumptuous fruit crops and forests of magnificence and have swept rich alluvial soil onto fields farmed to produce generous harvests. Of the means of using this river as a great force supplying energy, many remain today, but traces of hundreds of years of industry, large and small can also be seen for the sharp-eyed who know where to look. Hopefully this book has supplied many a clue.

BIBLIOGRAPHY
AND SOURCES

Aitken, J., *Making Passage to Perth* (privately published 1980)

Banner, J.M., *Braes o' Tullymet* (Perth and Kinross District Libraries, 1993)

Barclay, G.J., *The Cowie Line: A Second World War 'Stop Line' West of Stonehaven, Aberdeenshire* (Edinburgh, Society of Antiquaries of Scotland, 2005)

Barnard, A., *The Whisky Distilleries of the United Kingdom* (London, *Harpers Weekly* Gazette 1887, re-printed Edinburgh, Mainstream, 1987)

Bowler, D.P. and Cachart, R., *Tay Street, Perth: The Excavation of an Early Harbour Site* (Edinburgh, Society of Antiquaries of Scotland, Edinburgh, 1994)

Buczacki, Stefan, *Creating a Victorian Flower Garden* (London, Diamond Books, division of Harper Collins 1992)

Byrom, B., *Old Comrie, Upper Strathearn and Balquidder* (Catrine, Ayrshire, Stenlake Publishing, 2005)

Byrom, B. *Old Pitlochry, Strathtummel and Rannoch* (Catrine, Ayrshire, Stenlake Publishing, 2005)

Byrom, B., *Old Crianlarich, Tyndrum and Bridge of Orchy* (Catrine, Ayrshire, Stenlake Publishing, 2006)

Campbell-Preston, Lt.Col. R.M.T., *The Scottish Horse in South Africa*

Carnie, R.H., *Publishing in Perth Before 1807* (Dundee, Abertay Historical Society, 1960)

Cole, Sue, *Discovering Meigle* (locally published 2004)

Collier, Basil, *The Defence of the United Kingdon* (London, HMSO, 1957)

Comrie Women's Rural Institute, *Comrie Our Village* (1966)

Cooke, Anthony J., *A History of Redgorton Parish* (Dundee, Department of Extra-Mural Education, University of Dundee, 1984)

Dean, Marcus, and Miers, Mary, *Scotland's Endangered Houses,* (London, SAVE, Britain's Heritage 1990)

Dingwall, C.H., *The Hermitage: an Historical Study* (The National Trust for Scotland, 1995)

Ferguson, Naill *Dundee and Newtyle Railway* (Monmouth, Oakwood Press, 1995)

Finlay, W.H., *Heritage of Perth* (Perth and Kinross Council, 1994 and 1996)

Fleming, Maurice, *More Old Blairgowrie and Rattray* (Catrine, Ayrshire, Stenlake Publishing, 2006)

Forrester, David M., *Logiealmond* (Edinburgh, Oliver and Boyd, 1844)

Gow, I., *Scotland's Lost Houses* (London, Aurum Press Ltd, 2006)

Groome, F.H., *Ordnance Gazetteer of Scotland: a survey of Scottish topography, statistical, biographical, and historical, Vol.1* (London, William Mackenzie 1882)

Harting, James Edmund, *British Animals extinct within historic times* (Boston, J.R. Osgood and Co. 1880)

Hetherington, Sheila J., *Katherine Atholl 1874–1960: Against the Tide* (Aberdeen, Aberdeen University Press, 1989)

Hunter, T., *Woods Forests and Estates of Perthshire* (Perth, Henderson, Robertson and Hunter, 1883)

Hutton, G., *Bygone Scone* (Catrine, Ayrshire, Stenlake Publishing, 2006)

Jack, J.W., *Scott's View from the Wicks of Baiglie* (Perth, Milne, Tannahill & Methven, 1933)

Huxley, Thomas, *Exploring the Past in the Almond Valley* (Perth, Thomas Huxley, The Old Manse, Pitcairngreen 2005)

Keay, John and Julia (eds.), *Collins Encyclopaedia of Scotland* (London, HarperCollins, 1994)

Kennedy, J., *Folklore and Reminiscences of Strathtay and Grantully* (Perth, Munro Press, 1927)

Kerr, John., *The Robertson Heartland* (published by John Kerr)

Lang, Sir P.R.S., *Duncan Dewar, A student of St Andrews 100 years ago* (Glasgow, Jackson, Wylie and Co., 1926)

Lear, Linda, *Beatrix Potter, a Life in Nature* (London, Allen Lane Penguin Group 2007)

Macara, D., *Macara's guide to Crieff, Comrie, St Fillans and Upper Strathearn including excursions to every point and place of interest in the district* (Edinburgh, 1890s)

Macdonald Douglas, Ronald, *The Scots Book* (London, Alexander Maclehose, 1935)

Macmillan, Hugh, *The Highland Tay from Tyndrum to Dunkeld* (London, H. Virtue and Company, 1901)

Marshall, W., *Historic Scenes in Perthshire* (Edinburgh, Oliphant, Anderson and Ferrier, 1881)

Merritt, J.I., *Baronets and Buffalo, the British Sportsman in the American West 1833–1881* (Missoula, MT, Mountain Press Publishing, 1985)

Miles, Hamish, *Fair Perthshire* (London, John Lane, the Bodley Head Ltd, 1930)

Miller, James, *The Dam Builders, Power from the Glens* (Edinburgh, Birlinn 2002)

Mitchell, Hugh, *Pitlochry District – its Topography, Archaeology and History* (Pitlochry, 1923)

Moody, D., *Old Blairgowrie* (Blairgowrie Library, 1976)

Mundy, J., *A History of Perth Silver* (Perth, Perth Museum and Art Gallery, 1980)

Munro, D., *A Vision of Perth* (Perth, Perth and Kinross Libraries, 2000)

Murdoch, K., *Gask Parish Church 1800–2000* (privately published 2000)

Oglesby, R.E., *Scotsman in Buckskin: Sir William Drummond Stewart and the Rocky Mountain Fur Trade* (New York, Hastings House, 1963)

Paterson, Janet C., *Scottish Glass a Collector's Notes* (Edinburgh, Libraries and Museums Committee, 1958)

Paton, D., *Twixt Castle and Mart, the Story of Needless Road, a Suburban Street in Perth* (Perth, Perth and Kinross Council, 2005)

Peacock, D., *Perth: Its Annals and its Archive* (Perth, Thomas Richardson, 1849)

Perry, D.R. and Reid, A.G., *Pitmiddle Village and Nunnery* (Perthshire Society of Natural Science, 1988)

Reed, Nicholas, 'The Scottish Campaigns of Septimus Severus', (Edinburgh, *Proceedings of the Society of Antiquaries in Scotland*, Vol. 107, (1975–76),

Shaw, J., *Water Power in Scotland 1550–1870* (Edinburgh, John Donald, 2006)

Sinclair, D. McDonald, *The Blacksmith's Story, Reminiscences of Duncan McDonald, J.P.* (privately published 1986)

Small, John.W., *Scottish Market Crosses* (Stirling, Eneas Mackay, 1900)

The Statistical Accounts of Scotland, 1791, 1845, and 1950

Weir, Marie, *Ferries in Scotland* (Edinburgh, John Donald 1988)

Woolliscroft, David and Hoffman, Birgitta, *The Romans in Perthshire* (Perth, Perth and Kinross Heritage Trust, 2005)

INDEX

Illustrations are marked in **bold**